The Consumer's Guide to Organic Wine

THE CONSUMER'S GUIDE TO
Organic Wine

ROBERT JOHNSON, COMPILER
RICHARD PASICHNYK, EDITOR

ROWMAN & LITTLEFIELD PUBLISHERS, INC.

ROWMAN & LITTLEFIELD PUBLISHERS, INC.

Published in the United States of America
by Rowman & Littlefield Publishers, Inc.
4720 Boston Way, Lanham, Maryland 20706

British Cataloging in Publication Information Available

Library of Congress Cataloging-in-Publication Data

Johnson, Robert, 1960–
The consumer's guide to organic wine / Robert Johnson, compiler ;
Richard Pasichnyk, editor.
p. cm.
Includes bibliographical references and index.
1. Wine and winemaking. I. Pasichnyk, Richard. II. Title.
TP548.J67 1992   641.2'2—dc20   92–31699 CIP

ISBN 0–8476–7759–1 (cloth : alk. paper)

Printed in the United States of America

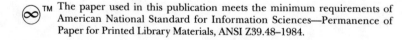

™ The paper used in this publication meets the minimum requirements of
American National Standard for Information Sciences—Permanence of
Paper for Printed Library Materials, ANSI Z39.48–1984.

Contents

Preface   ix

Acknowledgments   xiii

A Living, Fermented Health Food Beverage   1

Wine Terms, Tables, Tips, and Types   11

    Terms Commonly Used to Describe Organic Wines   11
    Contains Sulfites   17
    Contributors to Determining a Higher Quality Wine   21
    Why There Is a Government Warning on Wine   26
    Lead: "A Clear and Reasonable Warning"   27
    Does Daily Wine Consumption Make One an Alcoholic?   29
    Wine and Pregnancy   30
    Wine in Hospitals and Health Care Facilities   31
    Wine and Spirituality   32
    Types of Wine and Serving Suggestions   33
    Proper Storage of Wine   35
    Social Responsibility, Research, and Public Education   36
    Legislation and the Organic Wine Industry   38

U.S. Organic Wineries   41

    Amity Vineyards   42
    Badger Mountain Vineyard and Winery   43
    Bellerose Vineyard   44
    Blue Heron Lake Winery   46
    Briceland Vineyards   47
    Cameron Winery   48
    H. Coturri and Sons   49
    Fetzer Vineyards   50
    Fitzpatrick Winery   52
    Frey Vineyards   53
    Hallcrest Vineyards   55
    Hess Collection Winery   57
    Hidden Cellars Winery   60

La Rocca Vineyards   61
Las Montañas Winery   63
Nevada County Wine Guild   64
Octopus Mountain Cellars   66
Olson Winery   67
Orleans Hill Winery   68
Paul Thomas Winery   69
Paul Vineyards   70
Ponderosa Vineyards   71
Prager Winery and Port Works   73
San Pietro Vara Vineyard and Wine Company   74
Silver Thread Vineyard   76
Topolos at Russian River Vineyards   77

Importers and Distributors of Organic Wines   81

Chartrand Imports   81
Kermit Lynch Wine Merchants   86
Natural Wines Internationale   88
Organic Vintages   89
Organic Wine Company   91
Robert Haas Selections   94
Robert Kacher Selections   98
Terry Theise Selections   99
Weygandt–Metzler Importing   102

Conclusion: A Toast to a Healthier Society and Environment   105

Wine Tasting Notes   107

Domestic Reds   107
Domestic Rosés and Blushes   114
Domestic Whites   115
Domestic Sparkling Wine   120
French Reds   120
French Rosés   124
French Whites   124
French Sparkling Wines and Champagne   126
German Reds   127
German Whites   127

Italian Reds   127
Italian Whites   128
Conclusion   128

Bibliography   131

Index   141

About the Compiler   157

About the Editor   158

Producer, Importer, and Distributor Address and Phone List   159

Tables and Figures

Minerals in Wine Promoting Cardiac Health   2

A Summary of the Benefits of Wine   6

Logos of French Certification Organizations   14

French Certification Organizations   15

Ruling of U.S. Bureau of Alcohol, Tobacco, and Firearms on Organic
   Wine Labeling   18

Factors Determining a Higher Quality Wine   26

Types of Wine and Serving Suggestions   34

The Hess Collection   59

Classification of U.S. Organic Wineries   80

La Suvera, Pievescola, Italy   93

Association of German Prädikatswein Estates Upgrades Their
   Standards   100

Preface

"The Organic Revolution" has arrived, read the headline of the *San Francisco Chronicle* in April 1989. Some officials have estimated that the U.S. organic market is a $5 billion industry. One source reports a 160 percent growth rate over the past ten years. Wine industry officials also report an increasing demand for and availability of organic wine in the United States.

The first U.S. production of organic wine was in 1979. A little more than a decade later, at least 24 U.S. producers and 10 importers and distributors representing 40 French, German, and Italian producers are serving the growing consumer demand in the United States for chemical-free wine.

Wine occurs naturally and has been around as long as the grape. In its simple form, wine is "fermented grape juice." To produce wine, there need not be any intervention by humans; the broken skin of a grape will attract wild yeasts, which metabolize the grape and produce alcohol. An extensive body of research documents the positive role wine has played in society for more than 6,000 years. Because of its complexity, traditional use with meals, relatively low alcohol content, and associated sensory pleasures, wine is accorded a special place in many cultures and is viewed as a part of healthy lifestyles.

Wine is unlike other forms of alcohol. Most research studies have shown that moderate drinking (one to two glasses a day) of wine is beneficial to one's health. Gene Ford, author of *The Benefits of Moderate Drinking,* is one of several authorities who have written about this topic. In addition, two researchers (Pittman and Klein, 1989) discovered that wine is primarily consumed with meals in a family setting and "usually deemed appropriate in integrative, social enjoyment-enhancing situations." In a landmark study done at Kaiser Permanente and published in the *Journal of the American Medical Association*, moderate drinkers had an 8 to 10 percent increase in life expectancy and had a dramatic reduction in the overall rate of mortality. (Klatsky, 1981). The famous Framingham Heart Study found a lower rate of heart disease among moderate drinkers. When compared with controls—abstaining or heavy drinkers—moderate drinkers also had elevated levels of high-density lipoprotein (HDL) cholesterol, known to correlate with improved cardiovascular survival and reduced risk of arteriosclerosis (Freidman and Kimball, 1986). Other studies have shown a strong correlation between the per capita consumption of wine in European countries and reduced cardiovascular mortality (St. Leger and Cochrane, 1979). In comparative studies with nondrinkers and drinkers, a dramatic decrease in sudden cardiac death has been found among the drinking population (Renaud, and de Lorgeril, 1992; also see "60 Minutes," 1991). Salvatore Lucia, a famous authority on wine, has written several books on this subject, which include *History of Wine as Therapy*, *Wine and Health*, and *Wine and Your Well-Being*.

Terrance Leighton, a microbiologist at the University of California, believes that the proper use of red wine helps to fight cancer because one of its ingredients is quercetin, which is a benevolent mutagen. In a paper presented at the Chemical Society's Meeting in Dallas, Texas, 1989, he states, "when the quercetin-sugar bond is broken, such as in fermentation of grape juice to wine, quercetin is liberated. . . . Much the same process occurs in the human gut, and the similarity may be what makes quercetin one of nature's most potent anticarcinogens" (pp. 1–2). Leighton also adds that the agent is either not found or found only in low levels in white and rosé wines, and it is not found in beers or liquors.

June Forkner, health educator at San Francisco State University, has written several articles on the subject as well: "Wine: Your Key to a Healthy Heart," and "Should Wine Be on Your Menu?" Forkner wrote in her article on the role of wine in health and nutrition that red wine contains significant amounts of vitamins B and P. The benefits of these are reviewed in the following section. Many other benefits are documented on the proper use of wine, and several of them are reviewed in this book.

Unlike other books written on the health benefits of wine, this book is designed to provide consumers with information about proper use, and to serve as a guide for selecting and buying the highest quality organic, chemical-free wines. Two hundred of these wines are reviewed here, approximately half of which are domestic; the other half are imports from France, Germany, and Italy.

Many people have quit drinking wine because it gives them a headache, upsets their stomach, or has triggered an asthma attack; some have reported a burning sensation in the nose and throat. Charles Mitchell, coauthor of *Tainted Booze*, a publication of the Center for

Science in the Public Interest, states that about a million Americans have allergic reactions to sulfites, one of several common wine additives and preservatives. According to Mitchell, about 80 additives routinely are used in wine, including sugars, plastics, bases, acids, and several animal products: egg white, blood, casein, and collagen. Organic wine does not contain these additives with the exception of low levels of sulfites in some wines.

An equal or greater concern is the use of pesticides and chemical fertilizers that are applied in most conventional agricultural practices used today. Grapes are one of the most heavily sprayed crops. According to conservative estimates, seventeen insecticides, fumigants, and herbicides are used in wine as well as in table grape production. Don Flaherty, Tulare County, California farm adviser, states that they have been used and abused to such an extent in certain Central Valley vineyards that insects there have developed extreme resistance and cannot be killed with legal application rates. Even California Department of Food and Agriculture literature describes these chemicals as "very highly poisonous" (*Wine Spectator*, 1990). A number of insecticides have caused deaths among farm workers. These deaths have led to demonstrations and grape boycotts by table grape growers over the past several years, which were greatly inspired and led by Cezar Chavez, president of the United Farm Workers of America. And for good reason. He has voiced many examples of illnesses, deaths, and deformities that have resulted from pesticide exposure caused by working in the grape fields (Briseno, 1989).

Cornell University entomologist David Pimentel estimates that about 10,000 deaths among consumers and farmers are the direct result of pesticide poisonings each year (Pearce, 1987). Millions more in Third World countries have died because of pesticide-immune, malaria-carrying mosquitoes that have evolved as a result of conventional agricultural practices. A 1976 World Health Organization report stated that "evidence has . . . accumulated to show conclusively that resistance in many [mosquitoes] has been caused as a side effect of agricultural pesticide use" (Engenman and Pank, 1984). Mosquito resistance is only one example of how ineffective pesticides can be, and how unsafe this approach is.

The costs—monetary and environmental, as well as the flavor and balance of wine—of continuing with conventional agriculture are leading some wine giants, such as E. & J. Gallo, Buena Vista Winery,

Sutter Home Winery, and Fetzer, to join the organic movement. For example, Gallo, the world's largest winemaker, recently applied for organic certification on its 2,700-acre Ripperdan Ranch near Fresno, California, making it the largest grower of organic grapes. Gallo is encouraging its contract growers to adopt organic or sustainable agriculture as well. Some of these producers will not have certified organic wines because additives will be used, and therefore, the buyer should be cautious.

Wine drinkers deserve a high-quality product that is free of detrimental substances. And farm workers should be assured hazard-free working conditions. Therefore, this book was created to encourage such practices. It provides an industry profile of all organic wine producers known in the United States, as well as importers from France, Germany, and Italy. The wineries were each asked to provide a description of unique processes for making their wine, their location, and their motivation for using organic methods.

By supporting ecologically nurturing agriculture, such as organic methods, individuals can make a difference. In an economically based society, consumerism is the tool whereby we can change the world in which we live by how we spend our dollars. In striving to better our health, we must know (1) what forms of foods are most healthy, (2) what products are produced by health-conscious, life-nurturing practices, and (3) the proper use of these products. In the long run, we will all benefit. Consumer practices that truly benefit everyone, including our environment, represent a peaceful movement that provides solutions to society's problems and enhances the quality of life for all. Wine that is used properly and is organically produced is based upon this life-nurturing concept.

Acknowledgments

Much appreciation goes to Veronique Raskin, president of the Organic Wine Company, and Rusty Eddy, director of public relations for Glen Ellen Winery. They provided many of our industry contacts, contributed a section on organic wine production, and made invaluable suggestions. Both currently are board members of the Organic Grapes into Wine Alliance. The goal of the Alliance is to expand public education and develop high industry standards that U.S. wineries, as well as other industries, can follow. Many thanks also go to Richard Figiel, coauthor of *Dictionary of American Wine*, who contributed the introduction to the section on organic wine producers. And last, this book would not have been complete without the information submitted by the organic wine representatives who have chosen to be the forerunners of this new movement toward the preservation of life. Please support such good intentions economically. They are dedicated to nurturing the environment and providing you with the highest quality product: organic wine—a living, fermented health food beverage.

A Living, Fermented Health Food Beverage *

The use of wine to reduce tension, both physically and emotionally, is a valid usage and is widely recommended by those who have studied its effects. Wine should *not*, however, be consumed in great quantities, and then, dry red wine is superior to other forms when considering health. In one study, over an eighteen-day period, the use of moderate doses (4 to 8 ounces) of wine resulted in the enhanced retention or absorption (or both) of calcium, phosphorous, magnesium, iron, and zinc, more so than with deionized water or other alcoholic beverages.[11,22,23,24,25,26] Wine, unlike other alcohol, has more nutrients, including protein (24 or more amino acids), water-soluble minerals (manganese, magnesium, potassium, sodium, lithium, chromium, iron, etc.), and water-soluble vitamins (B and C); does not cause excessive water release (not diuretic); and is even considered a whole food.[2,16,22,23,24,30] Even a very toxic metal, mercury, which is sometimes found in grapes due to fungicides, is almost totally eliminated by the fermentation process.[5] Scientific evidence discloses that drinking moderate amounts of wine is beneficial to both mind and body.[11,16,22,23,34,37]

Alcohol, just one of the more than 300 components of wine, produces a wide range of effects on biochemistry and physiology. First of all, alcohol is not a foreign substance to the human body, which produces its own alcohol; alcohol has been observed by spectroscopic analysis on the breath of newborn babies.[30] Moderate doses of alcohol cause blood vessels to open (vasodilation), and can decrease the reabsorption of water by lowering the secretion of the "kidney-hormone" (antidiuretic hormone; ADH).[6] In contrast, the use of ADH has been beneficial in overcoming alcoholism.[35,36] The effects of both ADH and another hormone (renin), stimulated into balance during physical affection, lead to increased urine flow, causing a loss of water and salt (sodium and chlorine), as occurs with the ingestion of water but magnified.[6,30] In fact, alcoholism can create a condition similar to a kidney or uric acid disorder. Alcohol more commonly causes hyperuricemia, which generally results in the release of and limits the reabsorption of water,[23,30] causing a reduction of water-soluble nutrients, particularly B-complex,

---

* In this chapter, numbered references are used to document the scientific information. These references are found at the end of the chapter.

1

vitamin C, magnesium, calcium, and potassium. However, this is *not* the case with wine.[11,22,23,25,26,30] Because the adrenal glands, central nervous system, brain chemical (neurotransmitter) synthesis, and metabolism require these nutrients, the body and mind's biochemistry can become imbalanced as a result of alcohol abuse,[8,32,33] but not with the proper use of wine—in fact, the effects of wine are the opposite.[11,22,23,25,26,30]

Much evidence shows that wine produces both therapeutic and disease-preventive effects; other alcoholic beverages do not. In addition, research involving eighteen developed countries disclosed the fact that the availability of doctors is *not* a factor for producing lower rates of heart disease (i.e., ischemic); however, wine consumption *is*.[37] Alcohol (2 ounces or less per day), in general, lowers the risk of getting coronary disease, but wine in particular has properties that make it effective in this sense.[11,16,22,23,24,25,26,34,37] Some of these properties of wine increase the more beneficial type of cholesterol in the blood (high-density lipoproteins in serum), which helps remove the less beneficial sort of cholesterol (low-density lipoproteins).[34] Wine is a good source for trace minerals— more so than beer or spirits—particularly chromium (good source for the recommended daily allowance), deficiencies of which are a factor in causing heart disease (i.e., ischemic).[16] Vitamin P, which strengthens blood vessels, and thereby is a preventive against cardiovascular diseases, is also present in red wine.[11] Basically, the distinction is that beer and spirits are sometimes factors in causing disease,[7,12,13,15,29,30,32,38,39,41,42,43] whereas wine helps to prevent disease.[11,16,22,23,24,25,26,34,37]

MINERALS IN WINE PROMOTING CARDIAC HEALTH

Mineral	Concentration in wine (mg/liter)	Recommended dietary intake (mg/day)	% Dietary intake from 250 ml wine/day (8.4 oz)
Silicon, Si	29	3.5	143
Chromium, Cr	450	220	45
Iron, Fe	10	16	16
Potassium, K	800	3,300	6
Magnesium, Mg	60	305	5
Calcium, Ca	60	800	2

Source: D. June Forkner, health educator, San Francisco State University.

Wine can also improve the palatability of food, increasing adherence to diets, and has been used to treat anorexia and obesity. For people who are underweight, a 4-ounce serving before a meal can increase food intake by stimulating gastric acid secretion.[11,41] For people who are overweight, wine can reduce food intake if consumed with or after a meal by replacing calories of foods that are eliminated: i.e., reducing the amount of food eaten and then replacing the lost calories of those eliminated foods with a glass of wine can lead to consuming less food, thereby reducing weight.[11,18] Therefore, wine can help overcome extremes in body image and, as a result, improve self-esteem.

In a study of people in a home for the elderly, wine helped to induce sleep, especially for those who had trouble sleeping, and also increased interpersonal communication. Furthermore, both the tranquilizing and stimulating properties of wine helped the caretakers reach elderly patients and provide them with more services. The recommendation which arose from this study was that wine could help make those latter years of a person's life happier.[40] Therefore, aside from its nutritional benefits, wine might even increase longevity on this level alone.

Wine can reduce emotional and physical tension by a calming effect due to 1 or more of the over 300 congeners, of which only 1 is alcohol.[2,11,22] More than 1,000 years before the discovery of insulin, wine was prescribed to help overcome diabetes mellitus, and today many European and American clinicians prescribe dry table wines as part of a diabetic diet because it stimulates insulin secretion. In this context, dry red wine is best (0.2 grams sugar/4 ounces of wine), then white (0.4 grams), dry sherry (1.2 grams), rosé (1.3 grams), and dry champagne (1.8 grams); sweet kosher wines and dessert wines are not recommended for this treatment. Beer (13.7 grams carbohydrates/4 ounces of beer), light beer (5.5 grams), and distilled spirits (all carbohydrate) are not at all good for this purpose.[11,23] Furthermore, beer can destroy the microorganisms in the intestines (beer contains candida), which is part of many diseases; beer has specifically been correlated to intestinal cancers.[38] Both beer and distilled spirits are more often involved in increased aggressiveness, violence, and crime statistics.[7,43] So, dry red wine is superior because it is lowest in sugar and high in vitamin P, chromium, and iron; contains water-soluble vitamins and minerals; enhances nutrient and protein absorption; increases beneficial types of cholesterol (HDL); is a whole food; and has a protein (tyramine) that causes less of a reduction in

3

certain brain chemicals (cathecholamines).[2,6,8,11,13,14,16,22,23,24,25,26,27,34,37]

None of these facts is surprising in light of a single understanding: wine is alive with its own microecology. For people who have migraines or asthma, dry white wine may be better because red wine has more of an ingredient that can cause migraines (histamine).[10] This, however, is not the case with wines from poor European and Third World countries, which also have little sulfur dioxide.[2] By far, though, dry red wines from places that do not use chemicals in their production (typically poor countries or local organic farms) are a valuable addition to diet and health.

Those whose diets are high in protein, fat, or carbohydrates (or a combination of any of them) can destroy the microbiology in the intestines (increasing candida). Such individuals merely need to consume a high carbohydrate snack or meal—cookies, cake, candy, soda, bread, ice cream, etc.—to produce alcohol within their own system, even enough to become intoxicated.[17,18] People with diets like this are often rigidly opposed to the use of any alcohol even though scientific studies show the wide-range benefits of wine, and in spite of the fact that they produce their own alcohol internally.[4,5,20]

Better wines, according to scientific analysis, tend to come from poor countries, or local organic vineyards,[21] where they do not use chemical fertilizers, pesticides, additives, and catalysts that speed up the fermentation process. For example, Spanish wines contain less sulfur dioxide, and more manganese and lithium, among other things, than other countries' wines.[2] Poor countries that have *not* been involved in wars, especially the world wars, and therefore have little or no chemical industry, such as Spain, Portugal, and Argentina, offer some of the better wines. In contrast, wealthier countries with chemical industries, such as Germany, Italy, Belgium, and Angola, have gone so far as to add antifreeze to sweeten their wines. Even countries such as the United States, France, and Japan, with regulations that prevent the use of some additives, still most often produce wine with many additives. These substances are metabolized with vitamins B_1 and C, and can reduce intestinal flora and offset hormones. In the United States, however, there are some organic wines that are labeled as such.

Another way of determining whether a wine is good involves the use of our senses. Good wines are soft and velvety to the tongue's sense of touch, mildly sweet, fruity, full, and complex to the taste, and expansive and fruity to the sense of smell. When held up to light the wine bends and reflects it (opaque), and is fairly thick, causing drips that cling (rivulets) on the side of the glass. In contrast, wines that are not good are sharp and biting to the tongue and the nose, have a sharpness that is hidden by sweetness, are also bland or limited in taste, are watery, and are fairly clear or transparent. When a wine is not good, one easily gets tipsy or intoxicated and feels badly after consuming it.

In conclusion, when considering heart disease prevention and the proper stimulation of insulin (lowest in sugar), the best wines are dry and red. This advice is especially true when the wine has been aged five or more years, and comes from poor countries without a chemical industry or if the wine is organically produced.

Factors that contribute to a higher quality wine include measures of pH, sugar content, and the addition of sulfites. A higher quality wine has a higher pH level (lower acidity) for its category. Dry red wines are also improved by aging (five or more years) because this neutralizes some substances (aging denatures tannins and tannic acid, as well as enhances the balance of microecology and various wine congeners).[2]

The better quality wines in a given category are lower in sugar and higher in pH, because better timing in the fermentation raises pH, and sugar converts to alcohol and other components. Sulfites are used as an antioxidant and antiseptic, and to check the fermentation process. The lower the sulfite content, the better the wine is with regard to quality handling.[19] Quality handling basically involves any factor that prevents the contamination or oxidation of the wine (i.e., the timing of the process, technology that seals the wine off from air, bottling, sterilization, etc.), thereby eliminating excess sulfites. A lower sulfite content is also better health-wise because some people are sensitive to sulfites, which can cause allergic reactions or asthma attacks. To sum it up, a high-quality wine should have a higher pH, be lower in sugar for its category, and have little or no added sulfites, and a high-quality red wine should be aged.[2] This is more thoroughly examined in the section Contributors to Determining a Higher Quality Wine.

Alcohol, in the form of wine, can be used properly and beneficially, particularly if a person has a weight problem, and poor food or mineral digestion, absorption, or retention (or any combination thereof). Wine, particularly dry red, can enhance mineral absorption and retention, increase food consumption if used before a meal, and decrease food intake with, or after, a meal. Also, it is a preventive against heart disease, aids in a sound sleep, enhances interpersonal communication, reduces tension and anxiety, and is attributed with the components of a whole food. However, this is true only for modest intake, such as 4–8 ounces (120–240 milliliters) per day, not an entire bottle or more. In addition, people with eating disorders, such as anorexia, bulimia, and obesity, and also depression, should be very careful, for a tendency *may* exist for developing alcoholism.[41] Likewise, in rare cases some people may have developed diabetes as a result of alcoholism, and therefore, prescribing wine is not beneficial. The beneficial effects of wine are not surprising because of all beverages, wine is the only living drink, with the exception of cultured drinks, which do not possess the variety of living components (microecology) of wine. Alcoholic beverages other than wine are not complete foods and have been correlated to such human problems as disease (digestive system cancers and diseases) and violence.

"What constitutes a healthful diet?"* One part of the answer is: "wine should be on *your* menu."

A SUMMARY OF THE BENEFITS OF WINE

- Reduces emotional and physical tension and anxiety
- Enhances retention or absorption of nutrients
- Is higher in nutrients than other alcoholic beverages
- Helps to induce sleep
- Is a factor for lowering the risk of heart disease
- Can help in the treatment of eating and weight disorders
- Consists of more than 300 congeners, of which alcohol is only 1
- Can help in overcoming diabetes mellitus
- Is a whole food
- Enhances interpersonal communication
- Increases longevity

---

* For a more in-depth understanding of what constitutes a proper diet, see Rich Passion, *Nutrients for Love: A Nutritional Approach for Achieving Optimum Mental and Physical Functioning,* 1989. Tempe, Arizona: Loveglo & Comfort.

References

1. Amerine, M. A., and C. S. Ough. (1974). *Wine and Must Analysis*. New York: John Wiley & Sons.
2. Amerine, M. A., and C. S. Ough. (1988). *Methods For Analysis of Musts and Wines*. New York: John Wiley & Sons.
3. Amerine, M. A., et al. (1972). *Technology of Wine Making*. Westport, Conn.: Avi Publishing Company. (see also later editions)
4. Barker, L. M., editor. (1982). *Psychobiology of Human Food Selection*. Westport, Conn.: Avi Publishing Company.
5. Boakes, R. A., et al., editors. (1987). *Eating Habits: Food, Physiology and Learned Behavior*. New York: John Wiley & Sons.
6. Chruscel, T. (1982). "General Pharmacology and Toxicology of Alcohol." Pages 160–176 in F. Hoffmeister and G. Stille, editors. *Handbook of Experimental Pharmacology*, volume 55/III. New York: Springer-Verlag.
7. De Lint, J. (1978) "Alcohol Consumption and Alcohol Problems from an Epidemiological Perspective." *British Journal of Alcohol and Alcoholism* 13(2):75–85.
8. Ellingboe, J., and J. Mendelson. (1982). "Biochemical Pharmacology of Alcohol." Pages 209–237 in F. Hoffmeister and G. Stille, editors. *Handbook of Experimental Pharmacology*, volume 55/III. New York: Springer-Verlag.
9. Enkelmann, R., et al. (1984). "Quecksilberspuren in Most und Wein." ["Mercury Traces in Must and Wine"] *Zeitschrift fur Analytische Chemie* 317(3/4):478–480.
10. Feldman, J. (1983). "Histaminuria from Histamine-Rich Foods." *Archives of Internal Medicine* 143(11):2099–2102.
11. Forkner, D. (1982). "Should Wine Be on Your Menu?" *Professional Nutritionist* Spring:1–3.
12. Gad-Luther, I. (1980). "Sexual Dysfunctions of the Alcoholic." *Sexuality and Disability* 3(4):273–290.
13. Hennekens, C. (1979). "Effects of Beer, Wine and Liquor in Coronary Deaths." *Journal of the American Medical Association* 242(18):1973–1974.

14. Ho, A., and B. Kissin. (1976). "Drug-Induced Alterations on Alcohol Preference and Withdrawal." Pages 447–460 in D. H. Ford and D. H. Clouet, editors. *Tissue Responses to Addictive Drugs*. New York: Spectrum Publications.

15. Hopkins, A. (1981). *Epilepsy: The Facts*. New York: Oxford University Press.

16. Jennings, M., and J. Howard. (1980). "Chromium, Wine and Ischemic Heart Disease." *Lancet* II(8185):9–91.

17. Kaji, H., et al. (1976). "Autobrewery Syndrome—The Repeated Attacks of Alcoholic Intoxication due to the Overgrowth of *Candida* (Albicans) in the Gastrointestinal Tract." *Matera Medica Polona (Warszawa)* 4:1–7.

18. Lenz, H., et al. (1983). "Wine and Five Percent Ethanol Are Potent Stimulants of Gastric Acid Secretion in Humans." *Gastroenterology* 85(5):1082–1087.

19. Lichine, A. (1977). *Alexis Lichine's New Encyclopedia of Wines and Spirits*. New York: Alfred A. Knopf.

20. Logue, A. W. (1991). *Psychology of Eating and Drinking. An Introduction*. New York: W. H. Freeman & Company.

21. Loveglo, B. (1989). *Why Panic? Eat Organic!!* Tempe, Ariz.: Loveglo & Comfort.

22. Masquelier, J. (1978). "Vin et Nutrition." ["Wine and Nutrition"] *Annales de Technologie Agricole* 27(1):427–439.

23. McDonald, J. (1981). "Mixing Alcohol with Nutrition." *Professional Nutritionist* 13(3):3–6.

24. McDonald, J., and S. Margen. (1979). "Wine versus Ethanol in Human Nutrition, 2. Fluids, Sodium, and Potassium Balance." *American Journal of Clinical Nutrition* 32(4):817–822.

25. McDonald, J., and S. Margen. (1979). "Wine versus Ethanol in Human Nutrition, 3. Calcium, Phosphorus, and Magnesium Balance." *American Journal of Clinical Nutrition* 32(4):823–833.

26. McDonald, J., and S. Margen. (1980). "Wine versus Ethanol in Human Nutrition, 4. Zinc Balance." *American Journal of Clinical Nutrition* 33(5):1096–1102.

27. Mello, M. (1982). "Behavioral Pharmacology of Alcohol." Pages 175–208 in F. Hoffmeister and G. Stille, editors. *Handbook of Experimental Pharmacology*, volume 55/III. New York: Springer-Verlag.

28. Mezey, J., et al. (1975). "Endogenous Ethanol Production and Hepatic Disease following Jejunoileal By-Pass for Morbid Obesity." *American Journal of Clinical Nutrition* 28:1277–1283.

29. Murphy, W., et al. (1980). "Sexual Dysfunction and Treatment in Alcoholic Women." *Sexuality and Disability* 3(4):240–255.

30. Olson, R. (1979). "Absorption, Metabolism, and Excretion of Ethanol including Effects on Water Balance and Nutritional Status." Pages 197–212 in C. F. Gastineau, editor. *Fermented Food Beverages in Nutrition*. New York: Academic Press.

31. Passion, R. (1989). *Nutrients for Love*. Tempe, Ariz.: Loveglo & Comfort.

32. Pinhas, V. (1980). "Sex Guilt and Sexual Control in Women Alcoholics in Early Sobriety." *Sexuality and Disability* 3(4):256–272.

33. Projesz, B., et al. (1976). "Brain Excitability Subsequent to Alcohol Withdrawal in Rats." Pages 461–470 in D. Ford and D. Clouet, editors. *Tissue Responses to Addictive Drugs*. New York: Spectrum Publications.

34. Ricci, G., and F. Angelico. (1979). "Alcohol Consumption and Coronary Heart-Disease." *Lancet* I(8131):1404.

35. Robinson, A. (1980). "Neurophysins and their Physiological Significance." Pages 149–158 in D. Krieger and J. Hughes, editors. *Neuroendocrinology*. Sunderland, Mass.: Sinauer Associates.

36. Sahgal, A., and C. Wright. (1983). "Comparison of the Effects of Vasopressin and Oxytocin with Amphetamine and Chlordiazepoxide on Passive Avoidance Behavior in Rats." *Psychopharmacology* 80(1):88–92.

37. St. Leger, A., et al. (1979). "Factors Associated with Cardiac Mortality in Developing Countries with Particular Reference to the Consumption of Wine." *Lancet* I(8124):1017–1020.

38. Tuyns, A. (1979). "Cancer and Alcoholic Beverages." Pages 427–438 in C. F. Gastineau, editor. *Fermented Food Beverages in Nutrition*. New York: Academic Press.

39. Van Thiel, D., and R. Lester. (1976). "Alcoholism: Its Effect on Hypothalamic, Pituitary Gonadal Function." *Gastroenterology* 71:318–327.

40. Watkin, D. (1979). "Role of Alcoholic Beverages in Gerontology." Pages 226–245 in C. F. Gastineau, editor. *Fermented Food Beverages in Nutrition*. New York: Academic Press.

41. West, K. (1979). "Incorporating Alcoholic Beverages into Therapeutic Diets: Some Potentialities and Problems." Pages 257–262 in C. F. Gastineau, editor. *Fermented Food Beverages in Nutrition*. New York: Academic Press.

42. Wood, B., and K. Breen. (1979). "Thiamine Status of Australian Alcoholics." Pages 409–426 in C. F. Gastineau, editor. *Fermented Food Beverages in Nutrition*. New York: Academic Press.

43. World Health Organization. (1978). "Alcohol-Related Problems: The Need to Develop Further the W.H.O. Initiative." Report by the Director General. WHO Document EB 62/23, November 27. Geneva.

Wine Terms, Tables, Tips, and Types

Much confusion still exists about what organic is. As you will find in the following sections, organic wine producers state their own definition as well as standards for production. However, all growers share in the belief that the purpose of growing organically is to bring about a healthy soil, as well as to produce the highest quality product. Though most organic wine producers want to make a living by selling their products, their primary focus is to do it in a fashion that maintains a balance in nature, while avoiding the negative consequences of conventional methods, which may take years to develop, environmentally or physically.

Terms Commonly Used to Describe Organic Wines

The following terms serve to define different standards for production. One will find the wineries categorized according to these terms in the table, Classification of Organic Wineries, page 80.

Organically Grown

Grapes labeled with this designation have been grown without the use of synthetically compounded* fertilizers, pesticides, or growth regulators. Only microorganisms, microbiological products, and materials consisting of or derived solely from plant, animal, or mineral-bearing rock substances are applied by the grower. Some farmers may in fact grow their grapes organically according to this definition, but because they wish to avoid the red tape that goes with certification, or because they are too small to justify the additional costs, they choose to promote their product as organic without labeling it as such. However, it is important that the grower have some means to establish credibility,

---

* "Synthetically compounded" means "formulated or manufactured by a process which chemically changes a substance extracted from naturally occurring plant, animal, or mineral sources, excepting microbiological processes" (California Organic Foods Act of 1990).

such as a recommendation or confirmation by another organic farmer, organization, or credible source.

According to the California Organic Foods Act of 1990, all products sold as "organically grown" or similarly described must be produced, handled, and processed in accordance with the terms of the law, and must be labeled, invoiced, and represented as: "ORGANICALLY GROWN/PROCESSED IN ACCORDANCE WITH THE CALIFORNIA ORGANIC FOODS ACT OF 1990." This act, which became effective January 1, 1991, provides clear responsibility for enforcement of the state law and the means to support that authority. Labels that conform to the old law (Section 26569.11 of the California Health and Safety Code) could be used until January 1, 1992. In addition, part of the organic provisions of the 1990 Federal Farm Bill requires that all food products sold as organic (in operations with a gross annual income of more than $5,000) will have to be certified by October 1993.

In most cases, a farmer may simply "claim" to follow the letter of the law. However, California farmers promoting their wines as "organically grown" are now required under the Organic Foods Act of 1990 to register with their county agriculture commissioner.

Certified Organically Grown

Producers who label their wines with the "certified organically grown" designation abide either by state laws and codes or standards and rules of a private certifying organization. In Washington, for example, growers who wish to have their grapes certified by the state must follow Chapter 15.86 Revised Code as set forth in 16-154 Washington Administrative Code. Most state governments and certifying organizations require the farmer to wait through a transitional period, usually one to three years, before being certified.

In California, the transitional period has been one year, but the new legislation raises the transitional period to three years by 1993. In addition, the state law requires the certified organic farmer to not only abide by the law (i.e., must sign an affidavit), but also to complete a soil test and to provide accurate and detailed field maps, input records (i.e., source, amount, and location of all materials applied to all fields or production areas), and a complete audit trail (i.e., production and sales records for the operation that record the harvest date, amount harvested, sales dates, and buyers' names).

As of 1989, California Certified Organic Farmers (CCOF), a private, nonprofit certification organization, requires that all operations entering its certification program undergo a pesticide residue analysis as well as a fertility analysis. This pesticide residue analysis is generally only done once, and the primary test is for organochlorines. If conditions warrant, other tests can be done as often as necessary. Since 1987, CCOF has required a soil fertility test every three years. An annual farm visit by a trained contract farm inspector also verifies conformity to CCOF regulations. Certification is the consumer's greatest assurance that the purchased product is, in fact, organic. After the farmer has fully complied with the law, the wine then may be labeled as such on the bottle.

Certified Organically Grown and Processed

This designation signifies that the grapes in the wine are not only grown and certified by a government or private certifying organization as described above, but that the wine has been "produced and handled without any prohibited material or color additive having been applied" (California Organic Foods Act of 1990). Therefore, California wine producers who wish to label or market their product as "organic wine" or "organically grown and processed wine" cannot add any synthetic compounds, including sulfites. United States wineries that add sulfites to their wines made with organically grown grapes are limited to printing on their wine labels, "organically grown grapes" (see the next section, Contains Sulfites, for further explanation).

At this time, CCOF has no provisions for certifying wineries, although they do certify vineyards, which allows the winery's label to state that the wines are made with certified organically grown grapes. The organization does have a pilot project with two wineries, Hallcrest Vineyards and San Pietro Vara Vineyard, to develop standards for winery certification. Upon completion of such standards, wineries that do not add sulfites or other chemical additives to their wines will be able to label their wines with the "organic wine" designation.

In such European countries as Italy, Germany and France, wines labeled or certified as organic, naturel, or biodynamic (Demeter) may contain added sulfites, the majority of which are from naturally derived sources. Certified wines are the best assurance that added sulfites are minimal and from a natural source. In France, most organic wineries are certified by Nature et Progrès, Terre et Vie, or U.N.I.A. (National Interprofessional Union of Agrobiologists). The symbols below signify their seals of approval.

In a later section on organic wine producers, you will find that each has unique methods of producing wine. Therefore it is recommended that you read all of the sections on the wineries. In so doing, you will learn to what extent organic methods are used.

Some phrases that are found on some French organic wine and champagne bottles, in addition to a certification symbol, are the words *"culture biologique, sans produits chimiques, sans engrais chimiques, sans fongicides, ni herbicides, ni produits de synthèse."* This means that the wine is grown and produced without the use of synthetic chemicals, pesticides, herbicides, or insecticides.

Currently, lawmakers in California are being petitioned by a majority of U.S. organic wine producers, who have combined efforts and formed the group Organic Grapes into Wine Alliance (OGWA), to adopt French standards for the "certified organic wine" designation. The OGWA standards address wine processing in detail, recommend "certified organically grown" grapes, but allow claimed "organically grown" in accordance with state and federal laws. These standards differ from current state and federal laws by specifying what processed and processing agents and additives are recommended, accepted, tolerated, and prohibited. Standards include those for storing containers, cleaning methods, stabilizing agents, harvesting equipment, yeast, clarification and fining, coloring agents, acidification and deacidification, bottling practices, and the quality of corks used.

French Certification Organizations

European countries have an older and more fully evolved organic wine movement than does the United States. Given the centuries-old significance of wine in France, winemakers specifically look to the French and the organic guidelines established in the early 1960s by a professor of agronomy at the University of Angers.

Currently, approximately 250 organic winemakers in France follow the recommended guidelines. Most are members of various third-party organic farmer organizations, which certify their products. These agencies are administered and regulated under the control of the French Ministry of Agriculture. Depending upon the locations of their vineyards, these organic winemakers belong to or are supervised by Nature et Progrès, Terre et Vie, or U.N.I.A. (Union Nationale Interprofessionelle de l'Agrobiologie) All are government recognized or approved certification organizations.

— V. Raskin

Château Meric is a charter member of Nature et Progrès, largest of the independent organic certifying organizations in France. Nature et Progrès split from Lemaire Boucher in 1964. It is the first group whose standards were approved by the French Ministry of Agriculture and also aids its members through sales outlets in the Paris suburbs.

Transitional

As the name implies, this designation applies to growers who have farmed using conventional methods but have changed, or are changing, to organic methods, usually with the intent of obtaining the "certified organically grown" designation. The transitional period, as previously described, is usually one to three years. In 1993, the federal law will require a three-year period, which will override any state law. At the end of that period, the grower must submit to a soil test and present records of all substances applied to the field. Currently, there is no provision for "Transitional Organic" labeling in federal or state laws.

Biodynamically Grown

The concept of biodynamics was created near the beginning of this century by Rudolf Steiner in Germany and Switzerland and has now extended to many other countries. The term "DEMETER" is used as a certification mark in many countries for products grown by biodynamic methods. The Demeter Association sets the standards, and the Bio-Dynamic Farming and Gardening Association qualifies the inspectors. Biodynamic viticulture excludes the use of weedkillers, chemical fertilizers, and clone-type vinestocks. Its primary emphasis is on the building of healthy, living soil through the use of homeopathic (i.e., herbal) doses of specially prepared compost starter and field sprays. Farmers also pay attention to working with nature's complex ecosystems and the rhythms of the Earth and the solar system. For instance, Nicolas Joly, owner of a biodynamically grown vineyard in France, is concerned about the phases and positions of the Moon in relation to his plowing schedule. Vinification is accomplished as naturally as possible; it is never interfered with by the addition of yeast, cold processing, collage fining, or tight filtering (for an additional explanation, see Madame A. Joly's techniques of biodynamic viticulture, page 96).

This designation identifies wines produced from grapes that have been grown without the use of herbicides or pesticides, but may have been grown with commercial (chemical) fertilizers (i.e., synthetic nitrogen compounds, copper sprays). This designation should not be confused with organic growing methods. Although a farmer who produces grapes without the use of herbicides or pesticides may use some organic techniques, the consumer should not assume that this is the case.

For assurance, it is best to contact the producer to see to what extent organic methods are used. Encouraging producers to grow organically may eventually lead them to farm according to the above designations.

Contains Sulfites

Since 1988, the federal government has required warning labels on wines that contain more than 10 parts per million (ppm) of total sulfites. In contrast, the upper limit allowed has remained at 350 ppm. For people who are more sensitive to sulfites, an allergic reaction can result in headaches, hives, cramps, flushing, or other unpleasant experiences. The U.S. Food and Drug Administration reports that about 0.4 percent of the U.S. population, or around one million people, are highly allergic to sulfites. As few as 20 ppm may affect these individuals, while others within that group may not even consciously notice several hundred parts per million. Death has resulted from a sulfite allergic reaction in one rare case in the United States. (Tsevat et al., 1987; see also Dahl et al., 1986).

In organic wines, sulfites are used for the same reason commercial producers use them: to stop oxidation or deterioration of the wine, which may occur as soon as several years after bottling. White wines are particularly fragile. Red wines with a higher acidity can last longer without the additive, especially when special treatment is considered (see Frey Vineyards, pp. 53–55). Sulfur is also sprayed or dusted on vineyards by some growers to protect the grapes from a disease called Oedium. In addition, sulfites are burned or sprayed inside and outside casks as a disinfectant. Other sterilization methods are used by producers who want to avoid using sulfites. Most commercial wineries

Ruling of U.S. Bureau of Alcohol, Tobacco, and Firearms on Organic Wine Labeling

Section 105(e) of the Federal Alcohol Administration Act (FAA Act), 27 U.S. Code of Federal Regulations (CFR) § 205(e), authorizes the Bureau of Alcohol, Tobacco and Firearms (ATF), to issue regulations intended to prevent deception of the consumer, and to provide the consumer with adequate information as to the identity and quality of distilled spirits, wines, and malt beverages. Regulations that implement the provisions of section 105(e), as they relate to the labeling and advertising of wine, are set forth in 27 CFR Part 4.

There are currently no regulations specifically authorizing the use of the phrase "organic" on wine labels. There is no "organic wine" designation currently defined in the regulations which provide the standards of identity for wine. However, pursuant to 27 CFR § 4.38(f), labels may contain information other than the mandatory label information required by sections 4.30 through 4.39, if such information complies with the requirements of such sections and does not conflict with, nor in any manner qualify statements required by Part 4. In addition, information that is truthful, accurate, and specific, and is neither disparaging nor misleading may appear on wine labels.

In accordance with these provisions, ATF has approved labels that contain as additional information a statement to the effect that the wine was "made from organically grown grapes," as long as such information is truthful, accurate and specific. The bottler of the wine must submit evidence in support of the claim that the grapes were organically grown. Because the regulations in Part 4 do not define the term "organic," there is obviously potential for consumer confusion if the term is used by different wineries to mean different things. Thus, ATF requires the bottler to show that the grapes have met some established standard that entitles them to an "organic" designation. For example, ATF has approved labels that claim that the grapes have been organically grown in accordance with the provisions of state law, where the bottler has submitted evidence in support of that claim.

To the best of our knowledge, ATF has never approved a label containing the phrase "organic wine." An applicant for label approval who wishes to use such a phrase on a wine label bears the responsibility of showing, to ATF's satisfaction, that there is an established standard for "organic wine" with which the wine in question complies.

BATF Headquarters, Product Compliance Branch
650 Massachusetts Avenue, NW, Washington, D.C. 20226
Telephone (202) 566-7777

add between 80 and 200 ppm according to random U.S. Bureau of Alcohol, Tobacco and Firearms (BATF) tests. Although this amount appears high, some of the sulfites are broken down in the bottle; therefore, actual sulfite content can be much lower, as substantiated by tests. Some producers measure the sulfite content after their wines have been bottled.

Chemically Compounded Sulfites Versus Petroleum-derived Sulfur Dioxide (SO_2)

Chemically compounded sulfites are known as metabisulfites, which are sulfur atoms chemically combined with other elements. These include such forms as sodium bisulfite, sodium metabisulfite, potassium bisulfite, potassium metasulfite, and postassium metabisulfite. In contrast, petroleum-derived SO_2 is pure sulfur dioxide extracted from burned petroleum by-products, such as residues from smokestack filters. Most wineries in the United States that produce wine made with organically grown grapes use pure SO_2 in winemaking to prevent oxidation. The OGWA standards tolerate a limited addition of SO_2 gas diffused in water not to exceed 100 ppm total SO_2, or 30 ppm free SO_2 in wine, but they prohibit the use of the industry standard sulfiting agent, potassium metasulfite. However, according to an opinion rendered by the California Department of Health Services, SO_2 cannot be used in foods labeled organic. Therefore, for now, wines produced with SO_2 cannot be sold as "organic wines."

Fluidosoufre

In contrast to the California law, French standards governing organic winemaking limit use of natural sulfites—"fluidosoufre"—to fewer than 90 ppm in red wine and 100 ppm in white and sparkling wines. Most of their organic wines contain fewer than 80 ppm, which is less than one-third the industry's maximum allowance. Fluidosoufre is pure sulfur dioxide that has been isolated from mined sulfur without any chemical processing. By French standards, fluidosoufre is a naturally derived material, not a synthetically compounded one, and therefore organic winemakers are allowed to use it not only in France but throughout the European community. Organic wine producers in the United States who have adopted similar standards are members of the New York Natural Organic Farmer's Association (NOFA) and OGWA in California.

The overuse of sulfites can be detected by the bitter taste the wine leaves in one's mouth, as well as by a slight stinging sensation in the sinuses. White wines are more prone to oxidation and often contain more sulfites to prevent such from occurring. Sweet wines usually contain more because sulfites are added to stop fermentation and kill the yeasts before all the sugar is converted to alcohol. A fully balanced and ripened grape, in contrast, will not only produce a greater wine, but will more than likely require less antioxidants, such as sulfites and other additives.

French wine producer André Stentz uses an evolving technique that limits the use of sulfur. The process saturates the must with oxygen before fermentation so that anything in the grape juice that is susceptible to oxygen will oxidize before the fermentation and can then be removed during the fermentation. This is designed to produce a more stable product. Stentz has tried this method and is very pleased with the result.

Forms of vitamin C (ascorbic acid) have also been used to reduce the use of sulfites. More complete forms of vitamin C may prove to be more efficient still.

Interestingly, sulfites also are found in natural sources such as garlic, onions, and egg yolk. Analysis of a chicken egg at a research service in Healdsburg, California has shown that the egg contains 6 ppm sulfites. Is it possible these natural sources of sulfites, which are available organically grown, could be used for winemaking by being made into ash and purified through a filtration process?

Naturally Occurring Sulfites

Sulfites are believed to be a natural by-product of the fermentation process, depending on the yeast strain and type of grape. As yeasts ferment, the natural sulfite known as SO_2 often results, and in varying amounts, usually fewer than 10 ppm total, with an average of 3–7 ppm (however, there is a 10 ppm margin of error to the test). Climate conditions, kind of yeasts present, types of grapes, and other factors can boost the sulfite content to as high as 40 ppm. Yet most wine made from grapes without the use of sulfites contains fewer than 10 ppm. Some wines have "no detected sulfites" at all, which means that amounts are so small that they go undetected.

Most organic wine producers will tell you the total sulfite content of their wines, upon request. And several offer literature on the topic (e.g., Chartrand Imports and Organic Wine Company, among others).

Contributors to Determining a Higher Quality Wine

Several factors contribute to determining a higher quality wine. They include acidity (pH) and alcohol, sugar, sulfite content, naturally occurring sediment, growing and processing methods, and expert ratings. Human beings have very individual taste preferences and would likely disagree on which wine is best. However, most people agree on which wines are good. This section considers what factors tend to make a wine better and leaves individual or subjective concerns to each individual. It is not intended to be "the gospel" on quality but is meant to explore the subject as addressed by wine experts.[*]

Acidity (pH) and Alcohol

Acidity, measured in pH, can disclose the quality of a wine. The word acid is derived from the Latin word *acetum,* which means vinegar. The word vinegar comes directly from the French *vinaigre,* which means sour wine. We are all familiar with the idea of wine vinegar, which is very acidic, and in fact, wine does produce acid. The strength of an acid is designated by its pH, which ranges from 0 (strongly acidic) to near 7 (neutral). Because wine components (amines, etc.) are acids, wines are always acidic. Wine vinegar, which is far more acidic than any wine, is created by letting the fermentation process go unchecked. Therefore, the pH of a wine indicates how it was fermented and the expertise of timing in the fermentation process. A good wine will have a higher pH or be lower in acidity than a wine of lesser quality. Numerous wine encyclopedias make comments on this, such as,

---

[*] See the full citations for the following in the Bibliography: Amerine et al., 1972; Amerine and Ough, 1974; *Academic American Encyclopedia,* 1990; Grossman, 1974; Lichine, 1977; Ough and Amerine, 1988; Schoonmaker, 1978.

> Wine left too long to ferment [will produce] more acidity and tannin, and more of the unsuitable acids, which would prove objectionable later. (Grossman, 1974: p. 10)

> An excess of acetic acid in a wine is almost always evidence of poor or careless cellar-work. (Schoonmaker, 1978: p. 2)

A quality, high-alcohol (12 percent or more) wine will range between 3.25 and 3.8 pH, with the higher pH designating higher quality. Aging is a factor in lowering acidity in wines, particularly red, because aging changes some components (denatures tannins and tanic acid, as well as enhances the balance of microecology and various wine congeners). The most thorough book on winemaking, *Technology of Wine Making,* indicates that red wines improve with aging five or more years and white wines for two to three years. More specifically the authors say of red wines, "the best wines may improve in quality in the bottle for 10 to 30 or more years" (Amerine et al., 1972: p. 10). Some red wines are made to drink immediately and are typically fermented in steel casks. These wines are usually of lesser quality but are also inexpensive.This is also true of some white wines. However, quality white wines can also improve with age in the bottle as indicated in this same book. "Fine white wines are usually greatly improved by aging in the bottle for 2 to 3 years" (p. 387). Because the pH is designated at the time of bottling, the age of a red wine is a factor and therefore ideally the wine should be used about five or more years after vintage. Dry, very high-alcohol (17 percent or more) wines, such as dry sherry, will undoubtedly have a lower pH (higher acidity), whereas high-alcohol sweet wines, such as dessert wines, will have a higher pH (lower acidity) due to the neutralizing effects of the sugar. This does not mean that dessert wines are better than dry sherry; actually the opposite is true because the sherry has a lower sugar content, which is healthier. Each is simply in its own category, but again, each category's pH will be higher if the wine is of better quality. **Determining a higher quality wine therefore involves a higher pH for its category (type and alcoholic content) and this also entails its aging (particularly dry red wines).**

Sugar

Another consideration of quality in a wine is its sugar content because it is also a measure of quality fermentation. Sugars are converted into alcohol and other wine components in the fermentation process, and less sugar will be present in the final product if the wine was fermented to its full potential. "Fermentation is the result of chemical changes by which the molecule of sugar is split into two molecules of ethyl alcohol and two molecules of carbon dioxide gas. The gas escapes into the air and the alcohol remains" (Grossman, 1974: p. 10). Sugar should be considered along with pH and a wine's category. A lower pH should be accompanied by a lower sugar content.* Wines with a lower pH and less sugar are referred to as dry and have a higher percentage of alcohol. In contrast, a higher pH usually means that the sugar content is higher. Wines such as these are rosé and some white wines that are lower in alcohol, and they are not considered dry. Again, dessert and some fruit wines are in their own category in which a low pH and high sugar content occur together. Dry wines are generally healthier and are essential for persons who have diabetes mellitus or blood sugar problems but wish to drink wine. **In summary, the better quality wines within a category are lower in sugar and higher in pH.**

Sulfites

Sulfite content is another indication of the quality of wine. Sulfur checks the fermentation process so that the wine does not spoil (turn into vinegar), and this is why it is often used. Those producers who do not use sulfites have to be very meticulous in handling their wines. However, the addition of small amounts of sulfites does not make a wine unacceptable. Why an organic source of sulfur has not been used is puzzling. Garlic, onions, and egg yolks are all high in sulfur and could be made into ash and purified through a filtration process that would prevent any odor or taste in the finished wine. Sources such as these would allow wineries to

---

* Fermentation produces acids and converts sugar to alcohol. Therefore, more acid (lower pH) should be accompanied by less sugar—for a given category. In contrast, fermentation that is performed with expertise produces a greater pH (less acid) because of the timing and handling.

23

label their wines organically grown and processed, overcoming any strict definitions. Some wines that have naturally occurring sulfites in spite of how the wine is handled are still quality wines. About 5 to 10 percent of asthmatics are sensitive and could suffer an asthma attack. Excessive use of sulfites may also be the culprit for the headache during a hangover (increased histamines, etc.). Sulfites are also metabolized with vitamins B_1 and C, and can reduce intestinal flora, offset hormones, and/or imbalance brain chemicals (i.e., neurotransmitters and neuromodulators) (Kutsky, 1982; Wurtman and Wurtman, 1977–1985). The wines listed in this book have very low levels or no added sulfites, and would appear, and have been reported, not to cause such problems. **In conclusion, a lower sulfite content tends to indicate higher quality handling and is less likely to cause health problems for sulfite-sensitive consumers.**

Naturally Occurring Sediment in Red Wines

Most organic red wines are processed with a minimal amount of filtering so that the beneficial properties of the wine are not removed. A sign of a high-quality, properly aged wine is the formation of "tartrate crystals." According to *Technology of Wine Making*, filtration aerates the wine, which often leads to undesirable effects and the addition of more sulfites as an antioxidant (Amerine et al., 1972). Tartrate crystals form naturally and render the wine supple. By pouring the wine slowly, the bottle can be emptied down to the last drop, with only a light shadow in the glass. You may prefer to decant the wine to eliminate any fine residue. An added benefit of decanting a wine is the smoothness that results from allowing the wine to breathe. However, this is not true for all red wines and is more of a subjective concern. Wines, in general, start showing signs of this natural occurrence within two or three years of bottling. When you see this, take it as a sign of maturation, and that less processing has been used. This can also mean that the red wine has a greater nutritional value as well (more vitamin P from the skin residues and possibly fewer sulfites).

Organically Grown and Processed

Organic wines are potentially superior wines for several reasons. Amino acids, chelated minerals, and numerous vitamins are important to fermentation, and organic grapes have higher levels of these components (Allaway, 1975; Chen and Avnimelch, 1986; Schuphan, 1974) . Lower levels of nitrates and nitrites are another advantage because high levels could lead to undesirable characteristics in the wine. Furthermore, insecticides have been known to inhibit fermentation (Amerine et al., 1972). Therefore, organic grapes and methods allow for superior fermentation and the potential for better quality wines.

Expert Ratings

Ratings from experts who have tasted organic wines can provide insight into the quality of a wine that an amateur may not recognize at first. For example, one expert on French wines believes that, in general, Muscadet and Côtes-du-Rhône are the best organic white and red selections. Another example is *Wine* magazine (August 1989) which gave a 3-star or "Excellent Value" rating to a 1987 Tokay Pinot Gris from Alsace, a 1986 Puligny-Montrachet (Jean-Claude Rateau), Guy Bossard's 1988 Muscadet de Sèvre-et-Maine, Pierre Frick's 1986 Muscat from Alsace, and a 1986 Châteauneuf-du-Pape from Etienne Gonnet. Another expert explained that climatic conditions favor some parts of France more than others for organic wine growers, and that it is possibly no accident that the greatest concentration of organic winemakers is located in the warm, sunny regions of Provence where winds blow hard. These winds create a drying effect, which removes many of the problems caused by excessive humidity that affects growers in Muscadet, Burgundy, and Alsace, as well as some regions in Provence. This could well be a contributing factor behind their ratings as well.

Research indicates that consumers are not impressed with others' opinions, and too many judges and contests are often intended to promote certain wines. Therefore, expert ratings should not be the sole source for determining the quality of a wine.

Wine tastings and awards are another way to identify a high-quality wine. Awards, in addition to a description of the wine's attributes, are sometimes identified on "shelf talkers" in wine retail stores. If you are interested in attending a wine tasting in your area, a local wine distributor or retail outlet is one source of information for finding out who sponsors them.

FACTORS DETERMINING A HIGHER QUALITY WINE

pH (0–7)	Higher
Percent alcohol	Higher
Percent sugar	Lower
Sulfites (ppm)	Few to none added

OTHER FACTORS

Reds are aged 5 or more years and have naturally occurring sediment (tartrate crystals).

Wines are organically grown and processed.

If you are concerned about sulfite content or whether the vineyard is certified, see the section Classification of Organic Wineries. With regard to a wine being organic as a distinguishing factor, some winemakers feel that some precautions appear necessary. That is, a wine that is made with organically grown grapes does not by itself guarantee a high-quality wine because winemaking is a separate art. However, you can feel assured that the majority of organic wine producers not only use organic grapes, but also use the highest quality production standards. Expert opinions on the quality of these wines have been included for many of the wineries in this book.

Why There Is a Government Warning on Wine

As of November 18, 1989, a new warning label must appear on all alcoholic beverages. Wines and other alcoholic beverages that were bottled before this date can be sold without warning labels. With the passage of the federal Alcoholic Beverage Labeling Act, Congress was attempting to educate the consumer about the possible harmful effects of alcohol use.

The label makes no distinction between use and abuse of alcohol or its form (i.e., wine versus distilled liquor), nor does it consider the quantity of consumption at a given time. As we have discussed previously, wine can enhance health and nutrient absorption. This means that the proper use of wine will *not* cause health problems and birth defects.

Government Warning: (1) According to the Surgeon General, women should not drink alcoholic beverages during pregnancy because of the risk of birth defects. (2) Consumption of alcoholic beverages impairs your ability to drive a car or operate machinery, and may cause health problems.

As for impairing one's ability to operate a car or machinery, a U.S. National Department of Justice report indicated that about 2 percent of those arrested for driving under the influence drank only wine (1988, p. 1). In addition, the *Journal of Studies on Alcohol* reported that wine drinkers are the most responsible in their attitudes and behaviors concerning drinking and driving (Berger and Snortum, 1989; p. 238). Evidently, wine is a beverage of moderation consumed with meals, and people are opting to drink at home.

Lead: "A Clear and Reasonable Warning"

In mid-1991, the government released a study listing potentially dangerous levels of lead in wines, which included "some of the biggest brand names" (Deveny, 1991). These wines contained lead levels far higher than what is recommended for safe drinking water—15 parts per billion (ppb) or less. Some levels were almost as high as 2,000 ppb; however, the average was 80 ppb. Lower levels were found in domestic wines.

Wine industry representatives believe the test results are unnecessarily alarming because the U.S. Food and Drug Administration has not yet established an "acceptable level" for lead in wine. However, a government expert on lead states that "these levels of lead are excessive under any definition . . . . Even for an adult who isn't pregnant, I think they could pose some health risks" (Deveny, 1991). While lead contamination is a major health concern, Wells Shoemaker, a California pediatrician and chairman of the California Wine Institute's scientific advisory board, said wine is being harassed. "They don't bother to say that it has no more lead than the fruit juice people give their kids every morning. Grapes are no exception, but neither is chicken, broccoli, or potatoes" (Bullard, 1991).

In California, the state law forces vintners to give consumers a "'clear and reasonable warning' for any products that have lead levels exceeding one-half part per billion—which includes virtually all of the wines on the bureau's [Bureau of Alcohol, Tobacco and Firearms] list." However, the bureau is having difficulty establishing regulations, because patterns of wine and water consumption are different.

Some winemakers and government officials believe that the lead-foil bottle wrappers are the source of the lead. Not cleaning the lip of the bottle thoroughly before pouring the wine can result in some of the lead deposits from the wrapper ending up in the wine, they explain. An effective way to remove lead from the lip of the bottle before opening is to use a vinegar-moistened cloth to clean the residues off.

According to a two-year study by the bureau, lead levels in domestic wines averaged 58 ppb when samples were taken from wine poured over the lip of the bottle. Lead traces in imported wines were generally much higher, averaging 195 ppb. Therefore, the solution to eliminating lead that comes from wine wrappers is to clean the lip of the bottle thoroughly before removing the cork and pouring. The good news is that lead-foil wrappers are being phased out.

Another expected source of lead is groundwater, but this would only pose a threat from irrigated vineyards (see index for dry farming). In addition, organic wine should have less lead because composted and organic soils are excellent filters; only natural substances, which are more complex in nature, are applied to the soil.

Nitrate and sulfite forms of lead are the most toxic. Chemical fertilizers and fungicides, unstable and chemically active, are the most likely to form these toxic substances. Sources of lead are leaded petroleum, coal, and oil burning. Conventional agriculture requires more energy expenditure and machinery, including tillers, crop dusters, and chemical fertilizer appliers (i.e., both lead and nitrogen). In addition, chemicals require more energy to manufacture and are often derived from petroleum (i.e., they create nitric and sulfuric acids, leading to acid rain). Meanwhile, a healthy soil inhibits the movement of lead, and microorganisms, which are tolerant, form stable organic compounds (World Health Organization, 1989). This makes organic vineyards less susceptible to lead contamination.

Another factor that can contribute to lead contamination is location of the vineyard; that is, being downstream from the source. Organic vineyards are typically in remote regions, and lead pollution is worst near the sources of pollution, such as cities, factories, and machinery. Also, highland vineyards are better locations because they are cooler, have better drainage, more rain and are upstream from airborne and waterborne lead. Organic vineyards also retain more moisture and need little or no irrigation. Upland, dry-farmed, organic vineyards that require less machinery and use solar power are the least threat for toxic lead levels.

Does Daily Wine Consumption Make One an Alcoholic?

Malcolm McConnell states in his book, *The Mediterranean Diet*, that "Italians currently drink approximately 10 times as much wine as Americans [and yet] have one of the lowest rates of alcoholism in the world" (1987: pp. 69–70). In the United States, nine out of every ten people who drink alcohol do not develop a problem. The majority of the evidence suggests that people who have dependence-related problems (i.e., biochemical imbalances developed from lifestyle and hereditary factors) tend to use alcohol as a drug—as an escape—instead of as a food. These people who abuse other substances, such as cigarettes, sugar, coffee, drugs, and even food (i.e., those who overeat on a regular basis or eat mostly processed foods), are individuals who are likely to abuse alcohol (Gagley, 1981; Borg et al., 1987; Gunn and Farrington, 1982; Hippchen, 1976; Hippchen, 1982; Hoffmeister and Stille, 1982; Remond and Izard, 1979; Schauss, 1978; Schauss, 1980; Schauss, 1983; Schauss and Simonsen, 1979; Van Thiel and Lester, 1976; World Health Organization, 1978; Wurtman and Fernstrom, 1974; Wurtman and Wurtman, 1974–1984). Interestingly, a profile of middle-income Americans, as reported in the journal *Alcoholism: Clinical and Experimental Research,* showed that, of patients admitted to proprietary hospitals for alcoholism treatment, the majority did *not* prefer wine (Mendelson et al., 1982).

A ten-year study by Kaiser Permanente found that "persons reporting daily use of two drinks or fewer fared best; the heaviest drinkers (six or more drinks) had a doubled mortality rate." "Coronary disease mortality was significantly higher among nondrinkers" (Klatsky, 1981: p. 144). This U-shaped curve has been disclosed by many research studies. Moderate consumers have a reduced rate of mortality compared with nonconsumers and heavy consumers. According to an article published in *Recent Developments in Alcoholism*, "Clearly the results imply that moderate consumption, up to one to two drinks a day, is not detrimental and may in fact be beneficial for longevity" (La Porte et al., 1985).

Wine and Pregnancy

According to the associate chairman of the California Pacific Medical Center, Keith I. Marton, in an 1992 interview, dozens of studies have measured the effects of moderate alcohol consumption. The majority indicate beneficial effects, he states. "The fetal alcohol syndrome is directly correlated to heavy drinkers only. Meanwhile, the majority of studies show no differences between the offspring of nondrinkers and those of women who consume one to two drinks per day."

One study, in which 592 mothers participated, was published in the *British Medical Journal;* this study found "no detectable adverse relation" between a child's development and the alcohol intake of a mother who consumed up to 10 drinks a week. According to Charles Florey, an epidemiologist who is a professor at the University of Dundee in Scotland, "Whether we looked at consumption of alcohol before, during, or after pregnancy, we could find no adverse effect of drinking on the [children's] mental and physical development" (Forrest et al., 1991, pp. 22–26; see also Walpole et al., 1991; Mansson, 1991).

One researcher, Ann Streissguth, has carefully followed more than 400 children born to a variety of mothers. Interestingly, her initial analysis showed that children born to moderate drinkers (one to two drinks per day) had higher IQs than those born to nondrinkers. In contrast, multiple regression analysis data (which statistically accounts for various other risk factors thought to affect IQ) indicated that mothers who consumed more than two drinks per day during pregnancy resulted, on average, in a 5-point IQ loss for the child (Streissguth, 1990; also see Rosett and Weiner, 1984).

The wine industry, as well as the American Medical Association, does not advocate drinking during pregnancy, even though research has not shown that moderate drinking endangers the fetus. In fact, wine before a meal enhances the uptake and utilization of minerals and protein (i.e., chelated minerals) important to fetal development (zinc, calcium, iron, etc.).

Wine in Hospitals and Health Care Facilities

In 1985, a survey of wine service in hospitals indicated that "over half (52 percent) of the hospitals in the top 65 metropolitan areas of the United States offer a wine service to their patients."[*] In 1987, The Wine Institute reported the results of its survey: 68 percent of U.S. hospitals and other health care facilities currently serve wine or will be serving it in the near future. More recently, wine is finding a new place in nursing homes and retirement communities as part of food service. According to David N. Whitten, emergency department chief at Kaiser Foundation Hospital in Santa Rosa, California, surveys find that wine at mealtime results in higher patient morale and satisfaction. In an interview, he states, "The hospital food was judged more palatable and patients showed both a better appetite and improved sociability. I have recommended wine to patients for many years, as have many of my colleagues worldwide. Various controlled studies have shown that the pleasure and relaxation provided by a glass of wine stimulates socializing, one of the most important ingredients of good health, and one that may be increasingly beyond the reach of an elderly person with failing health and a shrinking social circle," he adds. Controlled experiments by Robert Kastenbaum and others have found that as little as 2 ounces of wine with dinner or an afternoon snack have a favorable influence on the self-esteem, mood, and sociability of older Americans. Some wine-drinking patients reported improved sleeping and blood pressure patterns. These findings were reported in the gerontological textbook *Alcohol and Old Age*. (Kastenbaum and Mishara, 1980; also see Guralnik and Kaplan, 1989)

---

[*] *A Survey of Wine Service in Hospitals in the Top Metropolitan Areas of the United States*, p.1.

Wine and Spirituality

Some people who read the Bible are against drinking any alcohol, yet wine's use is encouraged throughout. Noah, the most righteous of his generation, and his family drank wine. Wine was used as an offering at the altar, as indicated in Exodus 29:40, Leviticus 23:13, and Numbers 15:5–10 and 28:7–14. Deuteronomy 7:13 signifies that as a reward for obedience one's wine is blessed by God. Wine is also the reward for honoring God in Proverbs 3:10. Proverbs 31:6 says, "Let there be . . . wine for those that have heavy hearts." A wise statement that is, because wine is good for the heart and even helps prevent heart disease. One of God's wondrous deeds include "wine that makes glad the heart of man" (Psalms 104:15). In Ecclesiastes 10:19 we find that "wine makes one merry." Isaiah had vineyards and he says that God will give a feast of wine to all people in the Kingdom of Heaven (Isaiah 25:6). In the New Testament we find that Jesus was familiar with winemaking (Matthew 9:17, Mark 2:22, and Luke 5:37–38). He describes wine's use as an antiseptic for healing wounds along with oil (Luke 10:34). Vineyards were an integral part of the parable of the wicked husbandmen (Matthew 21:33–44). The first miracle Jesus performed was to turn water into wine, which according to a man familiar with wine, was better wine than he had been drinking (John 2:1–11 and 4:46). Jesus was called a "winebiber," evidently because he drank wine (Matthew 11:19 and Luke 7:34). And, for those who believe in Jesus, he says, "It is enough for a disciple that he be as his master" (Matthew 10:25). Wine was passed around at the Last Supper and the one who did not drink betrayed Christ. In 1 Timothy 5:23 we find: "No longer drink water, but use a little wine for your stomach's sake and your infirmities."

The Bible is part of the Koran and therefore this should also apply to Muslims. The Koran indicates that one should refrain from intoxicants (2:219), but moderate consumption of wine is not intoxicating. An intoxicant is defined as that which prevents one from daily prayer and devotion to Allah (5:90ff). Again, moderate consumption of wine uses Allah's gifts of life—grapes and the microecology of wine—and therefore is more a part of devotion than in conflict with it. In the chapter of Muhammad (47:15), we are told that there are rivers of delicious wine in paradise. In the Defrauders (83:25),

32

we are told that it is an exquisite wine, a pure drink that the nonbelievers are not allowed to drink.

Scriptural references to wine in other texts of major religions do not occur. In some, statements are made to the effect that one should refrain from intoxicants. However, wine used in moderation is not intoxicating—quite the opposite. Drinking wine is certainly not a "sin," but a blessing created by two God-given living things: grapes and the microecology that produces wine.

Types of Wine and Serving Suggestions

There are thousands of wine names around the world. Yet wines are generally classified into four categories: table (red and white), appetizer, dessert, and sparkling. The following is a brief description of each category's use. For a more detailed elaboration, see *The Story of Wine and Its Uses,* a publication of the Wine Institute. The serving suggestions indicated below are the traditional uses and need not be adhered to. Allow for your individual taste preferences.

Red table wines have a tendency to be dry and possess naturally produced tannins. For these reasons, they are best served with red meats, chicken, and fish, such as sea bass, halibut, and salmon, as well as with lighter meals, such as pasta, rice, cheese dishes, potatoes, etc. Alcohol content usually ranges between 12 and 13.9 percent. Varietal red wines are dominated by the flavor of the grape variety that gives each its name. These include Barbera, Cabernet Sauvignon, Carignane, Charbono, Gamay, Gamay Beaujolais, Merlot, Petite Sirah, Pinot Noir, and Zinfandel. Red wines are best served at room temperature between 65° and 70°F. This will help to bring out the full flavor.

Traditionally, white wine is served with chicken, fish (such as flounder, cod, and white fish), and other lighter meats. Some of the heartier, fuller bodied varieties can accompany game birds and other dark foods with distinctive flavor. White wine also goes equally well with cheese dishes, pasta, crepes, and so forth. Alcohol content normally ranges between 10 and 13.9 percent. White wines that contain at least 75 percent of the named grape are called varietal. These include Chardonnay, Chenin Blanc, French Colombard, Gewürztraminer, Grey Riesling, Pinot Blanc, Sauvignon Blanc (or Fumé Blanc), Sémillon, and White Riesling (or Johannisburg Riesling). White wines are usually served chilled and are best at around 55°F. This is the temperature they usually reach about one hour after being placed in the refrigerator. Older dry whites are better served at 60° to 65°F, like reds; this allows the aged character to come through more fully.

Appetizer wines, or aperitifs, usually accompany snacks, hors d'oeuvres, or soup as a first course to a meal. The most commonly known appetizer wine is sherry. Others include wines that are blended with natural herbs or fruit flavors such as special natural wines and vermouth. Alcoholic content usually ranges between 15 and 20 percent. Appetizer wines can be served either chilled or at room temperature, but are more often served chilled like white wines.

Dessert wines, as the name implies, are distinguished from other wines by their sweetness, and are often served as a dessert after a meal. Dessert wines include Angelica, cream sherry, several Muscats, and ports. They usually contain between 17 and 21 percent alcohol. Dessert wines can also be served either chilled or at room temperature, but the latter is recommended to enjoy the finer qualities.

TYPES OF WINE AND SERVING SUGGESTIONS

Food or Course	Type of Wine
All fish, pasta, cheese dishes	White wine, unless the food has been cooked in red wine or sherry
All meat, pasta, grains, potatoes	Red wine, although white goes equally well with poultry and other white meats
As an aperitif	White wine without food. If red is preferred, early maturing types of dry reds with higher alcohol levels
As dessert	Sparkling wine (less dry than brut), sweet white still wine, late harvest, or port

Sparkling wines are bubbly as a result of a second fermentation, sometimes within the bottle. Champagne is the most commonly known type. Sparkling wines have often been reserved for festive occasions, but current research indicates that they are being used more commonly. Dry sparkling wines can also be served as an accompaniment to an appetizer, and sweet ones with desserts. Sparkling wines contain between 10 and 13.9 percent alcohol. They are best served chilled at around 45°F, which helps to slow the release of the bubbles.

When the salad is served as a separate course, one usually drinks nothing with it. Sometimes salad is served with the main course, and usually a bite of bread between wine and salad will cleanse the palate.

Beyond the above suggestions is the culinary artist in each of us. Feel comfortable in experimenting with the various varieties of wines and get to know each distinctive flavor. Then use a little imagination when considering which wine would enhance the subtle flavors and spices of a given dish. Like a master chef you may create something that is not traditional but exquisitely savory. Bon Appetit!

Proper Storage of Wine

Wine is less subject to spoilage than most food so long as four factors are considered: bottle position, temperature, light, and absence of vibration. Good wines are sealed with corks, and therefore should be stored on their sides to keep the cork moist and tight against the bottle neck. If a cork dries and shrinks, the bubbles will escape from sparkling wine, and all wines will become subject to oxidation and vinegaring. The ideal temperature range to store wine is between 55° and 60°F, but wine will endure 70°F, so long as the fluctuation in temperature is kept to a minimum. Wine storage should also be kept well away from any heat source, including outside walls, especially south and west walls; a north wall is best. Dampness is not a concern if there is a flow of air. Dampness and no draft can lead to mold growth on corks and labels if the wines are binned. Wine is spoiled (oxidized) by long exposure to direct sunlight or daylight balanced (full-spectrum) fluorescent light, so all long-term storage should have none of either. Constant agitation also causes wine to age prematurely. Therefore, long-term storage (one month or longer) should be away from the vibrations of heavy motors, street traffic, and the like.

In summary, wine should be treated with tender loving care. After all, it's a living food. Placing it in its optimal environmental conditions will keep the microecology intact, thereby allowing it to reach its full potential, and yielding a most pleasant, life-enhancing beverage.

The following chapter describes each organic winegrower's unique methods and motivation for producing the most healthy, environment-friendly as well as palatable wines.

Social Responsibility, Research, and Public Education

Several private and nonprofit professional groups, organizations and associations provide information and educational materials on wine's role in health, and the importance of social responsibility. They are as follows.

The American Wine Alliance for Research and Education (AWARE) is a public, nonprofit corporation dedicated to providing a balanced, comprehensive view of wine's role in society and advancing scientific research on health and safety issues. They are also leaders in the development of educational programs and socially responsible initiatives, and provide an international resource center. For more information contact AWARE, 244 California Street, Suite 300, San Francisco, California 94111, telephone (415) 291-9113.

Americans for Safer Beverages, a project of the Center for Science in the Public Interest (CSPI), provides information on cancer-causing chemicals contained in alcoholic beverages. Two of CSPI's alcohol policy publications are *Tainted Booze* (80 pages, $3.95) and *Chemical Additives in Booze* (113 pages, $4.95). The Center also provides consumer information on organic foods as well as organizes political reform on issues such as organic farming. They also publish the *Organic Food Mail Order Suppliers Directory*. They can be reached at 1501 16th Street, NW, Washington, D.C. 20036, telephone (202) 332-9110.

The Demeter Association is a national organization for the certification of the products of biodynamic agriculture. Their standards for evaluation are similar to those used worldwide. Inspections are carried out by experienced biodynamic growers whose qualifications to do certification work are affirmed by the Bio-Dynamic Farming and

Gardening Association (B-D Association), which is responsible for education, advisement, publishing, and research in biodynamics in the United States. The B-D Association also supplies the Bio-Dynamic Preparations for compost and field sprays. The two organizations work closely together. The Demeter Association can be reached at 4214 National Avenue, Burbank, California 91505, telephone (818) 843-5521. The B-D Association can be reached at Post Office Box 550, Kimberton, Pennsylvania 19442, telephone (215) 995-7797.

Loveglo & Comfort, a public service, educational organization, was formed in 1989 to provide consumers and scientists with new understanding of our "Living Universe." Interdisciplinary research concerning humankind's role in this universe and how one may optimally interact in it has been continually ongoing for nearly two decades. They have published several books regarding nutrition's role in achieving optimal health, and are currently preparing long-awaited interdisciplinary works. If you would like to be notified of publications, write to Loveglo & Comfort, Post Office Box 88, Tempe, Arizona 85280. Loveglo & Comfort also started the Organic Connection, a source for those who wish additional information about the organic wines or producers mentioned in this book. For more information, write to Post Office Box 88, Tempe, Arizona 85280. Please include a self-addressed, stamped envelope.

The Society of Medical Friends of Wine seeks to stimulate scientific research on wine, develop an understanding of its beneficial effects, and encourage an appreciation of the conviviality and good fellowship that are part of the relaxed and deliberate manner of living that follows its proper use. They can be reached at Post Office Box 218, Sausalito, California 94966-0218.

The Society of Wine Educators formed in 1977 to encourage and improve information about the many aspects of wine, wine history, wine appreciation, viticulture, wine geography, winemaking, and wine service. This wide scope encompasses all activities related to the enjoyment of wine and the exchange of information and ideas for teaching others about wine. The society includes members who teach or write about wine at the academic and trade levels, as well as consumers who have a genuine interest in wine and wine education. For information on how to become a member, write them at 132 Shaker Road, East Longmeadow, Massachusetts 01028, telephone (413) 567-8272.

The Wine Institute's goals are to improve, protect, and promote the California wine industry. They maintain one of the country's finest wine libraries for use by its members and accredited authors. In addition, they offer a variety of information for the consumer and researcher, available upon request. They are titled as follows:

- Study Links Moderate Alcohol Consumption to Healthier Aging
- A Scientific Look at Wine
- The Sale of Wine in Restaurants
- California Wine Facts
- California is Wine Country: A Tour Guide of California Wineries
- Social Responsibility and Drunk Driving
- The Pleasures of Wine with Food
- The Story of Wine and Its Uses
- Wine and America
- Wine in Food Service and Health Care
- The Sale of Wine in Stores
- Code of Advertising Standards
- Issue Alert: What's in the New Label? (Government Warning)
- The California Wine Industry: Some Statistical Highlights
- Selected Sources of Wine and Grape Statistical, Economic and Marketing Information

For more information, contact The Wine Institute at 425 Market Street, Suite 1000, San Francisco, California 94105, telephone (415) 986-0878.

Legislation and the Organic Wine Industry

Several sources can provide information dealing with legislation and the organic wine industry. They are described as follows.

California Action Network (CAN), founded in 1977, works with any citizen or group who is interested in pesticide reform in agriculture. Of all the pesticides in the world, 10 percent are sprayed on California's farmland, with grapes—the most heavily sprayed crop—faring the worst. CAN has a sincere interest in helping to bring organic methods to grape production for this reason. Recently, that has meant working with winemakers to achieve uniform legislative definitions of "organic wine."

38

They can be contacted at Post Office Box 464, Davis, California 95617, telephone (916) 756-8518.

California Certified Organic Farmers, Inc. (CCOF) is a good source for information about organic farming certification standards because their standards are used by the majority of U.S. grape producers of organic wine. A copy of their *1991 Certification Handbook*, which includes a brief summary and the actual text of the California Organic Foods Act of 1990 (AB 2012) is available for a $10 fee. They can be contacted at Post Office Box 8136, Santa Cruz, California 95061-8136, telephone (408) 423-2263.

Organic Grapes into Wine Alliance (OGWA; previously the California Organic Wine Alliance) formed in 1989 to promote the production of wine from organically grown grapes. In an effort to standardize international and North American definitions for "organic wine," OGWA members spent more than a year translating, reviewing, and finally adopting their own production standards based on the French organic wine standards. They are currently involved in recruiting wineries interested in organics and in developing a media plan and a resource library for the press. They hope to be directly involved in both state and federal organic legislation. For more information, contact the Organic Grapes into Wine Alliance, 54 Genoa Place, San Francisco, California 94133, telephone (800) 477-0167. Copies of the OGWA organic wine standards are available for a $10 fee.

U.S. Organic Wineries

For some winegrowers, organic viticulture is nothing new. They have always managed their vineyards organically, simply because they farm the way their parents and grandparents did, before synthetic agricultural chemicals came into use. But these traditionalists are few and far between, especially in the United States. As a "movement," organic wine is just becoming established and organized. The first American-produced organic wines did not appear until the early 1980s.

Perhaps one reason for the late blooming of organic production in the wine business is that, in some ways, winegrowing does not appear to fit the premises of organic agriculture very well. The organic ethic tells you to grow the plant varieties best adapted to your site—but these do not necessarily make the best wine, and quality-minded winemakers often try to grow grape varieties on sites that stretch beyond their adaptable range.

The people involved in growing wine grapes organically tend to come into the business either with a wine-first orientation, or an organic-farming-first orientation. This does not mean they follow different practices, but within the scope of organic winegrowing, they may have their own agendas.

In Europe, where the organic wine scene is much more developed than in the United States, the motivation is primarily environmental. Organic farming is an obligation to the Earth and the life upon it.

In the United States, organic wine producers are more likely to be motivated by health issues. This has brought sulfites to the foreground of discussions aimed at establishing standards for making organic wine. The addition of sulfur dioxide to wine, as a preservative, has really caused the only significant difference of opinion among organic wine producers. They have come to accept the European standard, permitting limited addition of fluidosoufre—earth extracted and naturally derived sulfur dioxide. But some winemakers choose not to use it.

Thankfully, there will always be some differences of philosophy and style—all part of the diversity that makes wine so fascinating. In 1990, associations of grape growers and vintners on the West and East Coasts adopted specific standards that essentially mirror those in Europe. The stage is set for a dramatic increase in the number of organic vineyards and wines, building on the following pioneers.

Amity Vineyards

Amity Vineyards, Amity, Oregon, in addition to being internationally recognized for the quality of their wines, is the producer of Eco-Wine, Oregon's first certified organically grown, sulfite-free Pinot Noir. Myron Redford, Amity Vineyards' winemaker, said their first goal was to make a good Pinot Noir, so they chose a vineyard that had a proven track record for quality fruit, which also happened to be organic. "Our own Italian prune orchard at home is organically certified, [therefore] our desire to produce an organic wine is a natural extension of that interest." Redford also adds, "I think that people who are sensitive to sulfites or just prefer sulfite-free wine should have the benefit of wine produced by a winery well known for quality. . . . I was convinced that with good grapes and careful cellar practices we could get a good Pinot Noir in the bottle without sulfites and we did!"

The grapes for their wines are grown at the Cattrall Brothers Vineyard in Amity, which has been growing grapes organically for more than a decade, and was certified by Oregon Tilth, a private certifying organization, in 1990. During the label-approval process, U.S. BATF certified that the Eco-Wine was sulfite free. This is a requirement under Oregon's organic law, which is unlike that of California or France. Redford states, however, that he sees nothing harmful with the addition of sulfites: "they are naturally produced at low levels during the fermentation process." Nevertheless, he was challenged to see if he could make a good sulfite-free wine for those people that want or need them.

Amity Vineyards' wines are labeled "Eco-Wine" because of their total ecological package. Not only is the wine certified organically grown, but the bottles are rewashed, the labels are made of 100 percent recycled paper, and the capsules are made of nonleaded aluminum foil.

Badger Mountain Vineyard and Winery

Badger Mountain Vineyard and Winery is on a south-facing slope in the Columbia River Valley, Washington's finest viticulture area. Warm summer sun, deep volcanic soil, and water from mountain snows are essential to the character of their wines. They produce 25,000 cases of wine annually and presently tend to more than 80 acres of organic wine grapes.

   Their new, on-premises winery, completed in 1989, is outfitted with state-of-the-art American, German and Italian processing equipment, including 75,000 gallons of refrigerated stainless steel tanks. Four hundred oak barrels accommodate their barrel-fermented Chardonnay alone.

   In 1989, Badger Mountain Vineyard committed to 100 percent organic viticulture, while striving to maximize their natural resources. For years their grapes were sold to buyers such as Chateau Ste. Michelle, while they watched others make wines from their premium grapes. As of 1991, they were the only state-certified organic vineyard and winery in Washington. The desert climate consisting of cool nights and long sunny days makes for quality, balanced wines.

The photo on the right shows Badger Mountain behind the vineyards

The photo on the left is a close-up of their state-certified organically grown Chenin Blanc vineyards

Badger produces five varieties: Chardonnay, Sevé, Mountain Blush, Dry Riesling, and Johannisburg Riesling. The Chardonnay is aged in oak and is balanced with hints of fruit. The Dry Riesling is a dry wine with a fruity finish. The Johannisburg Riesling is done in the traditional German style. Sevé has been described as possessing aromas of figs and a slight hint of grass. The flavor is dry but

graced with a character that is rich and full-bodied. It contains 60 percent Semillon, 30 percent Chenin Blanc, and 10 percent Gewürztraminer and Riesling. Tom Stockley, *Seattle Times* wine columnist, finds the Séve "an enjoyable sipping wine . . . and very pleasant for the price." They add on average no more than 50 ppm sulfites, therefore abiding by the organic industry standard of fewer than 100 ppm. Badger wines are now being sold throughout the United States, as well as in Japan.

Bellerose Vineyard

Bellerose Vineyard, near Healdsburg, California, was founded in 1978 in the Dry Creek Valley, one of northern Sonoma County's most historic ranches where grape growing and winemaking began more than a century ago. The 45-acre ranch and the establishment of Bellerose Vineyard provided the Richard family a place to settle down and pioneer the development of Bordeaux-style blends of Cabernet Sauvignon, Merlot, and Sauvignon Blanc. Charles Richard, owner and winemaker, decided that a vineyard and winery offered a synthesis of a lifelong interest in the arts and in the land.

Richard's vineyard management is based on the practice of "sustainable agriculture." Richard sees himself in the role of steward or caretaker of the land. "Sustainable agriculture . . . does not deplete the soils or people," he adds.

On a Saturday morning it is not unusual to find Richard out in the vineyards behind his team of Belgian draft horses, Rowdy and Chucky, working the land. "Agriculture is the heart and soul of Sonoma County," he says, "and the horses are a symbol of the traditional art of farming." Richard believes that it is possible that these are the only horses used in

vineyard cultivation in the nation. In describing why he uses horses, he explains, "The horses are gentler on the tilled soil than the tractor." In addition, they are more maneuverable on the slopes, eat hay grown on the vineyard's land, and their manure nourishes the vines.

At Bellerose Vineyard, the emphasis on quality begins in the vineyards, where much effort has been directed to matching grape variety's rootstock to the appropriate soil type. Their wines reflect a traditional approach to winemaking and are handcrafted in every respect. Bellerose produces a Cuvée Bellerose Cabernet Sauvignon made from grapes that are organically grown in accordance with the California Organic Foods Act of 1990. Bellerose applies only natural fertilizers and has used organic methods since 1984. They do use a judicious amount of potassium metabisulfite as an antioxidant in their wines.

Production is at no more than 6,000 cases annually, 75 percent red and 25 percent white. The Sauvignon Blanc is barrel-fermented in Nevres oak for up to seven months, and the reds are fermented in 60-gallon Center Forest oak barrels up to twenty months.

Wine varieties include Cabernet Sauvignon, Malbec, Merlot, Cabernet Franc, Petit Verdot, Sauvignon Blanc, and Sémillon. All vintages of Cuvée Bellerose since 1984 are designated and labeled by the proprietor as organically grown. Their other wines are made with 70 to 80 percent proprietor-grown grapes (also organically grown), with the remaining grapes purchased from commercial grape producers. However, they are not labeled with the same designation.

Blue Heron Lake Winery

Blue Heron Lake Winery is presently in transition toward converting its 24 acres of grape vines to organic. It is located in the hills of Wild Horse Valley, which is partly in Napa County and partly in Solano County. At the 1,400-foot elevation it is due east of Carneros. In December 1988, the U.S. BATF, recognizing its unique qualities, granted a separate

appellation designation for Wild Horse Valley. The ocean controls the weather. Cool Pacific winds cross the Carneros region and climb the hills to the valley. This results in temperate summer afternoons, uniformly cool nights, and a slow ripening of the grapes. The topsoil is a rocky, volcanic type unique to the valley. Low yields—less than 2 tons per acre in the eleventh (1990) growing season—are characteristic. The berries and clusters are small with high skin to juice ratios. The fruit is intensely flavored with excellent balance of sugar, acid, and pH.

Blue Heron began its operations in 1985 and produces two grape varieties: Chardonnay and Pinot Noir. In 1985, the Chardonnay grapes that they did not use were sold to Acacia Winery; since then they have used all the fruit for their own Blue Heron Lake Winery label. Their 1988 Spring Chardonnay harvest took place during September, with wonderful balance of sugars, acids, and ripe fruit flavor. For this 1988 vintage, 1,393 cases were made.

Since they began operations, their winemaker, David Mahaffey, has refused to use any type of insecticide in the vineyard. Although he has sparingly used herbicides, alternative techniques are being explored to control weeds. He hopes to be certified organic by 1993, considering the three-year transitional period required by the California Certified Organic Farmers Association (CCOF). According to Mahaffey, only judicious amounts of sulfites are used, and no more than 100 ppm— which abides by the organic standards of the Organic Grapes into Wine Alliance (OGWA).

In an interview, Mahaffey explains that he is going organic because he believes in the "méthode ancienne," French for "the ancient method" of making wine. He feels that we must act as "stewards of the land," and therefore has assumed the responsibility "to nurture it to a healthier state than when it was found."

Quality and taste are no sacrifice. It's been said that California Chardonnays suffer from too much "sameness." Mahaffey states, "I know that our unusual soil, cool growing season, and small yields can produce wines of unique aromatic and mineral flavors. The clusters are hand sorted so that only perfect fruit is crushed."

Robert M. Parker, Jr., publisher of the *Wine Advocate,* describes their 1988 Chardonnay as "light straw-colored, with an emerging bouquet of apples, minerals, and oak. . . this medium- to full-bodied, surprisingly intense, yet firmly structured, crisply styled wine is suggestive of a premier cru Chablis." Although most California Chardonnays have a tendency to fall apart after two to three years of the vintage, Parker believes this wine may have the necessary depth and overall balance to last for several years. *California Grapevine* described it as "above-average quality. Highly recommended." Ron Wiegand, writer for *Restaurant Wine,* also had praise: an "excellent value" wine.

Briceland Vineyards

Briceland Vineyards has several wines that are labeled with the designation, organically grown grapes. They feel strongly that sulfites are a preservative and that, therefore, there are few "organic wines." They are experimenting with wines with no sulfites and use as little as possible in their wine.

Currently Briceland offers CCOF-certified organically grown White Riesling, Chardonnay, Cabernet Sauvignon, and Pinot Noir. The vineyard that produces their certified organic grapes, Dennison Brothers of Anderson Valley, Mendocino County, California, has been farmed organically since 1978 and became CCOF-certified in 1983.

ORGANICALLY GROWN GRAPES

1988

MENDOCINO COUNTY
CABERNET SAUVIGNON

Anderson Valley—Dennison Vineyard

BRICELAND

V I N E Y A R D S

PRODUCED AND BOTTLED IN HUMBOLDT
COUNTY BY BRICELAND VINEYARDS
5959 BRICELAND ROAD • REDWAY, CA
95560 • BONDED WINERY 5284
TABLE WINE • CONTAINS SULFITES

Briceland also makes two wines from organically grown grapes from vineyards that have not yet been certified: Humboldt Sauvignon Blanc and Humboldt Brut Sparkling.

Briceland Vineyards is very small, producing about 1,000 cases per year. They are located 6 miles east of Highway 101 on the road to Shelter Cove, between Ukiah and Eureka, California.

Cameron Winery

Located south of Portland, Oregon, is Cameron Winery, producer of fine certified organically grown and processed wine. John Paul, winemaker, buys his grapes from the Cattrall Brothers Farm, a small 8-acre vineyard that has been farmed organically since 1980. Driving south from Portland to the winery, visitors pass through green forested hills and small Oregon townships. The vineyards are situated in the Eola Hills where the climate and conditions are similar to those of the French Burgundy region.

Paul specializes in producing a limited quantity of Pinot Noir. He uses wild yeast, which he thinks yields a much more complex wine. In accordance with the purity codes set by the Oregon Tilth, a private organic certification organization, nothing is added to this wine, including acids, fining agents, and sulfites. After aging in French oak cooperage for ten months, the wine is pushed out of the barrels with nitrogen and bottled directly.

Paul says he produces wines the organic way because he believes in the concept. In addition, he states, "I want to be in on it right from the ground up, so I can help influence the standards." When commenting on other organic standards, he adds, "The French model is a good one . . . [and] I think defined and limited sulfites should be allowed in organically grown grape wine." Yet he chooses not to add them to his Pinot Noir.

H. Coturri and Sons

H. Coturri and Sons is a 5-acre family operation that produces an average of 3,000 cases of wine annually. Their vineyards are at an altitude of 750 feet on a steep rolling hillside in Sonoma County, California.

Winemaker Tony Coturri explains that they grow their grapes organically because "the grapes are of much higher quality, and the acid, sugar, and other components of the wine are more evenly balanced. . . . There's no sense in putting harmful things in the ground," he adds, referring to pesticides, herbicides, and chemical fertilizers.

Special farming techniques include the use of cover crops and a bacterial system (The Bio-System™) for the soil. Cover crops attract beneficial predators as well as produce an abundant source of nitrogen in the soil, which is extremely beneficial to the vineyards. The application of a bacterial system to the soil adds beneficial microorganisms that enhance nutrient absorption and availability.

Wines from H. Coturri and Sons do not contain chemical additives of any sort. Tests by the U.S. BATF confirm that their wines contain no detected sulfites. In addition, they are unfiltered and unrefined, and are fermented with their own natural yeast. Though their wines are not certified organic, Coturri will happily provide an affidavit stating that their wines are produced according to the definition for organically grown described in this text. Coturri states that they do not certify their wines because they have always produced their wines organically. "We want to be known for producing great wines, not just because our wines are organic. Besides," he adds, "today's certifying groups allow for the use of sulfites, and we wish not to be classified with those that do." Certifying regulations will come and go, he insists, but their winemaking will always be produced with the highest quality in mind. In all the years of making wine, Coturri has

COTURRI

1989

Sonoma Valley

ZINFANDEL

PRODUCED AND BOTTLED BY
H. COTURRI & SONS LTD, GLEN ELLEN, CA
GRAPES GROWN AT CHAUVET VINEYARDS, SONOMA
ALCOHOL 14.7% BY VOLUME

Chauvet Vineyards is located one mile south of Glen Ellen on Sonoma Highway. It is owned by Blythe and Robert Carver. The vineyard is ten acres planted solely to Zinfandel, half old vines in 1935 and half newer vines planted in 1976. The old vines give character and body to the wine while the newer vines give fruit flavors and higher yield. The wine produced from this vineyard lends itself to many adjectives: full-bodied, intense, fruity, good color; but basically this wine reflects what used to be called "Zinfandel". Our grandfather or "Nono" would call this wine one that goes to your stomach not to your head.

H. Coturri & Sons use only natural yeasts in fermentations, no chemicals or additives are introduced nor is the wine filtered or fined. Wood cooperage is utilized exclusively in fermentation and aging. These wines will drop sediment and we recommend decanting.

GOVERNMENT WARNING: (1) ACCORDING TO THE SURGEON GENERAL, WOMEN SHOULD NOT DRINK ALCOHOLIC BEVERAGES DURING PREGNANCY BECAUSE OF THE RISK OF BIRTH DEFECTS. (2) CONSUMPTION OF ALCOHOLIC BEVERAGES IMPAIRS YOUR ABILITY TO DRIVE A CAR OR OPERATE MACHINERY, AND MAY CAUSE HEALTH PROBLEMS.

never lost a barrel because of not using sulfites. He says, "The key is keeping the operation on the proper scale, using good cooperage, and keeping the barrels topped."

Wine varieties include Zinfandel, Cabernet Sauvignon, Pinot Noir, and Albarello (a red blend). Albarello is an Italian word that means low, pruned vines. All their wines are fruity with a dry finish. The Zinfandel and the Pinot Noir are aged in French oak barrels for two years, the Cabernet Sauvignon for three years, and the Albarello for one year.

What do the critics think? For one, Coturri's wines are top-rated by *Parker's Wine Buyer's Guide*, which states that they are "remarkably rich [and] complex . . . [and] show every indication of being able to age well for up to a decade." Rod Smith in the *San Francisco Chronicle* agrees; he says that Coturri's wines are "good, often superb, but the absence of sulfites makes them a little different from wines we've all gotten used to. However, it doesn't seem to affect their age worthiness."

Fetzer Vineyards

Fetzer Vineyards of Mendocino County is a family-owned, fully integrated wine grower, producer, and sales marketing company focusing on the premium segment of the wine industry. They are well known for their wines, producing more than 2 million cases per year. Fetzer has plans to double this amount within the next three years. Of all their 1,300 acres of vineyards, 34 percent or 437 acres is solely dedicated to organic farming methods with the rest being farmed using integrated pest management (IPM) practices.* And they are adding more than 100 acres of CCOF-certified organic grown vineyards a year. Eventually, the company hopes to farm all of their acres organically.

At Fetzer Vineyards, their motivation for pursuing the organic approach is based on the concern for the safety of their children and families, preservation of the land and water resources for future

---

* IPM is a multisystems approach that involves aspects of modern conventional agriculture as well as those attributed to more ecological methods. It incorporates detailed pest and disease monitoring, novel uses of machinery and technology, and the use of the most benign pesticides possible. Pesticides are used only when warranted to obtain economically acceptable crop levels.

generations, safety of their employees, a desire to make the highest quality wine possible, and economic benefits. They feel that to continue with their success in the wine industry, experimenting with organic techniques makes sense.

Fetzer is also known for a showcase organic garden, which yields more than 85 varieties of apples, 40 kinds of peaches, 30 types of ornamental flowers, 16 herbs (including 6 types of basil and 10 varieties of oregano), 15 varieties of edible flowers, 25 varieties of lettuce, and more. Encouraged by the results of organic farming in their garden, Fetzer began experimenting with organic grape growing in 1987 at their Redwood Valley Home Ranch. Currently, 130 acres of Zinfandel, Sauvignon Blanc, and Cabernet Sauvignon are planted on this isolated property. It was certified organic by the CCOF in 1989. Their Valley Oaks Ranch Vineyard primarily produces Chenin Blanc, Chardonnay, and Cabernet Sauvignon varietals and was certified in 1991. Their experimental vineyard consists of 5.4 acres on the Valley Oaks Ranch. All the information gathered in this vineyard, as well as information on organic techniques, is being shared with grapegrowers and wineries throughout the world, including Australia and New Zealand. The University of California—home to some of the finest research professors in the United States—is also monitoring the project and using their research.

Other Fetzer-owned vineyards that are certified organic by the CCOF include the Blue Heron Block on the Valley Oaks property (80 acres), the Fairbairn Ranch near Hopland (21 acres), and the Kircher Ranch, located between Ukiah and Hopland (121 acres).

Consumers are demanding high-quality, chemical-free produce, and Fetzer is addressing those demands with organic grapes. In the future, as the fruit from their organic vineyards obtains the quality they believe it will, they will produce an organic wine as well. Because for Fetzer, as for the rest of the California wine industry, quality wines and a quality lifestyle are the key to the future.

Fitzpatrick Winery

Fitzpatrick Winery began operations in 1980 and currently offers facilities for food and lodging in addition to their wines. They have developed their products, their image, and their marketing methods over the past decade, and as a result, have become a unique, highly integrated small winery operation in the wine industry.

In addition to his commercial operations, Brian Fitzpatrick grows organic grapes in the granitic sandy loam soil of the Sierra Nevada foothills on 40 acres of Fitzpatrick Hill, which offers unique and varied growing conditions. Topography and tree density up to 2,500 feet have resulted in microclimates. Fitzpatrick's 40 acres are California-certified organic, and all farming practices follow the guidelines set forth by the CCOF. Fitzpatrick has been actively involved with OGWA, and as the Chair, has helped to develop high standards for other organic wine producers to follow.

Wines they produce from certified organically grown grapes include their Eire Ban, a Sauvignon Blanc, an estate-bottled Cabernet Sauvignon, Coloma Canyon Vineyard Cabernet Sauvignon, and Sierra Dreams, a Blanc de Noir. Their estate-bottled Cabernet Sauvignon is neither fined nor filtered, but aged in French oak barrels, then bottle aged for two years before its release. *Seattle Times* wine columnist Tom Stockley says he "fell in love with the deeply hued,

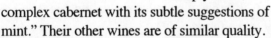

complex cabernet with its subtle suggestions of mint." Their other wines are of similar quality.

Fitzpatrick believes that farming without synthetic fertilizers, chemical pesticides, and herbicides constitutes the basics of what is allowable. "But quality organic wine," he adds, "is no longer based solely on what you don't do but demands creative practices of rebuilding the soil to a healthful state which in turn will feed the plant." A phrase that Fitzpatrick uses to describe his premium wines is "Uncork the Magic." It has become their trademark (unregistered) and has been printed on every piece of literature, including their case boxes, since 1983.

Fitzpatrick also feels that to pursue the winegrape tradition as a livelihood "requires a paradoxical balancing of vision and perseverance. Ten years after, although a sense of deep satisfaction claims our heart of present, the detailed visions of the future excitedly drive us forward. Our toils with Mother Earth are truly our pleasure and sanity. Sharing these fruits of labor with our family, friends, and customers brings us the ultimate satisfaction."

Frey Vineyards

At a time when the rest of the wine industry is worried about neo-Prohibitionism and declining wine consumption, Frey Vineyards has developed the market for organic wines and has inspired other wineries to follow suit, as well as expand production. In 1980 they could not even give their wine away. Now they produce 14,000 cases a year and have won numerous medals.

The Frey family, which includes eight sons and four daughters, lives and works at the winery, producing a wide range of varieties to meet the growing health concerns of wine drinkers. Every step of the grape-growing, winemaking, and marketing process is handled by a family member. They use no synthetically derived compounds anywhere in the process, from the vineyard to the bottle. Jonathan Frey explains that "a healthy soil creates a healthy plant. Healthy plants are much more resistant to disease, fungi, and pests. In turn, animals and humans who eat healthy plants will theoretically be more resistant to disease and be healthier." Frey wines are commonly found in health food stores in California as well as supermarket chains, and at prices that are competitive with commercial wineries.

Paul Frey filling the wine press with grapes

Frey's 145-acre ranch has an elevation of 1,000 feet and is in the upper reaches of the Russian River watershed near the Mendocino National Forest. This location is remote and keeps the vineyard isolated from atmospheric pollution, as well as protected from other vineyards' pesticide applications.

Frey wines are not only made from CCOF-certified organically grown grapes, but are naturally processed in accordance with the California Organic Foods Act of 1990. People allergic to sulfites will find Frey wines of particular interest because naturally occurring sulfites are extremely low (1–4 ppm). Frey's varieties are "less likely to cause common allergic reactions such as congestion," reports the March 2, 1989 issue of the *Wall Street Journal*. In addition, Frey's winebottle capsules are made of an attractive plastic, rather than the lead–aluminum alloys that leave a deposit on the rim and likely end up in the wine if the rim is not thoroughly cleaned.

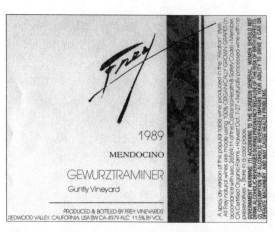

Because no sulfur is added during the winemaking, Frey applies some additional precautions and techniques to prevent air contact and oxidation. Also because sulfite-free wines are more fragile, the winery recommends special storage. The whites should be kept at 50°F or less, whereas their red wines can be treated like any other red, aged at 52° to 55°F.

Frey presently produces six organic red wines—Zinfandel, Cabernet Sauvignon, Syrah, Pinot Noir, Organic Red, and Carignane—and five organic white wines—French Colombard, Blush, Sauvignon Blanc, Estate Bottled Late Harvest Sauvignon Blanc, and Gewürz-traminer. Their Gewürztraminer was sampled by Pope John Paul II at a dinner in his honor during his visit to the United States in 1987. *Seattle Times* wine columnist Tom Stockley also states that "the Gewürztraminer from Frey, an '87, was one of the best domestic examples of that variety I have tried in years. It was brimming with spicy fruit, but fairly dry, much in the style of the great Alsatian wines." In a tasting of 20 wines, it was his first choice for the best of the bunch. Other tasters agreed as well. Also unsurprisingly, their 1988 Syrah won a silver medal at the Mendocino County Fair. According to a wine columnist for *The Wine Spectator*, "the current-vintage wines from Frey are surprisingly attractive. . . . Right now anyone who insists on drinking wines that are pure as can be should stick to reds and try to find those from Frey Vineyards." No wonder they are so popular in many states across the country.

Hallcrest Vineyards

Hallcrest Vineyards was founded by Chafcc Hall in 1941, who was widely recognized as one of the pioneers in the modern winemaking world. Hallcrest wines were served at such world-renowned establishments as the Fairmont Hotel, Top of the Mark, and the Waldorf Astoria in New York City. The last vintage under the Hallcrest label was produced in 1964 when Hallcrest retired. In the late 1970s, the site was reopened as Felton-Empire Vineyards, which in 1987 was sold to the Schumacher family. Located a half mile from the small town of Felton, Hallcrest Vineyards currently produces just under 16,000 cases annually and is easily the fastest growing winery in the Santa Cruz mountains.

Hallcrest feels that growing wine grapes without the use of chemicals is an important environmentally conscious step. Therefore, they have released a line of wines made from certified organically grown grapes: Estate White Riesling (CCOF-certified), Napa Valley Sauvignon Blanc (a blend with 16 percent Sémillon), and El Dorado Barbera, the grapes of which come from George Ritchie's Vineyard. For those who

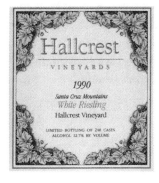

wish to enjoy the varietal fruit flavor of wine without the alcohol, Hallcrest released some organically grown, nonalcoholic juices: California Muscat and Sparkling White Zinfandel. All of these wines contain less than 70 ppm added sulfites.

The Organic Wine Works Label. Hallcrest also has released a line of premium certified organically grown wines that are produced without added sulfites: à Notre Mer (a nonvintage white wine), Chardonnay, Fumé Blanc, Sémillon, California White Zinfandel, Barbera, Merlot, Pinot Noir, and à Notre Terre (red wine blend). À Notre Terre means, "to our Earth." These wines are distinguished from those with added sulfites by The Organic Wine Works label. The Fumé Blanc has a smooth, fruity body with a soft, lush finish, and the Sémillon has a

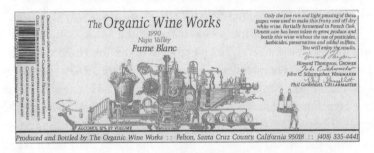

characteristically fresh, fruity body with a clean finish. Only the free run and light pressing of the grapes are used to make these two soft, semi-dry white wines. They are partially fermented in French oak puncheons and bottled with utmost care to avoid oxidation. In the interest of a cleaner environment, Hallcrest has made the package from materials that are recyclable or biodegradable. The capsules are made from nonleaded aluminum foil.

The Organic Wine Works wines are grown by Howard Thompson in Napa Valley, and produced and bottled by John Schumacher, the winemaker, and Phil Grossblatt, the cellarmaster. They feel confident that you will enjoy these wines for their premium quality as well as for their environmental and health benefits.

Hess Collection Winery

For more than ten years, Hess Vineyards on Mt. Veeder in the Napa Valley has focused on establishing itself as a producer of exceptional-quality, premium Cabernet Sauvignon and Chardonnay grapes. The original winery began in 1903, when award-winning wines were made by Theodore Gier. Over the years, the facility was expanded as the first Napa Valley winery of the Christian Brothers. In 1986, Donald Hess obtained this historic winery and began a major renovation to integrate traditional and modern winemaking techniques.

Hess bought three vineyard properties in Napa Valley from 1977 to 1980, totaling more than 900 acres. Two of the three properties had 60 acres (combined) of existing vineyard. From 1977 to the present, they have planted an additional 225 acres and will plant another 100 acres soon. The third property was virgin soil for grapes, and they now have about 95 acres of vines on it, all under organic cultivation. A serious effort is underway to grow vines using only natural, organic farming practices. They use no synthetic chemicals on this 95 acres, though they do use elemental sulfur in a formulation that is approved by CCOF. The vineyard blocks on the other two properties are being phased into organic farming. They are using permanent cover crop and no herbicides or insecticides. It will take them one more year to complete the transitional

Hess Vineyards on Mt. Veeder

phase for CCOF certification. Association with members of OGWA in California, in addition to the CCOF involvement, has also helped Hess to develop organic production standards in accordance with certification guidelines.

The objective of Hess has been to produce Cabernet Sauvignons that will age well for an extended time. Their powerful, concentrated flavors and aromas are characteristic of mountain grapes. In the reds, intense black currant and cassis aromas and flavors are the hallmark of Mt. Veeder grapes. For their Chardonnays, the winery tends to strive for complexity and richness, as well as a good balance and a palate-cleansing tartness in the finish. The whites have a crisp style with sound structure and balance.

THE **HESS**
COLLECTION
NAPA VALLEY CABERNET SAUVIGNON
1988
PRODUCED & BOTTLED BY THE HESS COLLECTION WINERY
NAPA, CALIFORNIA, USA
ALCOHOL 12.5% BY VOLUME

Both reds and whites are aged in French oak barrels; the whites for six to nine months and the reds from eighteen to twenty-two months. Barrel fermentations add pleasant dimensions of richness and depth. To ensure that the wines do not pick up too much oak flavor, tastings take place frequently.

Hess describes the challenge of growing grapes in the mountains. The development and farming costs, he says, are higher and the crop yields are much lower than on the valley floor. He hopes that the long-term benefit will be realized in the special qualities of the grapes grown on these hillsides. No doubt this is the reason why Hess is establishing a reputation as a producer of outstanding premium varietal grapes.

In addition to wine, Hess opened a permanent exhibit of artwork that he has acquired over the past twenty years. One hundred and thirty paintings and sculptures by contemporary European and American artists are now open to the public. They include Francis Bacon, Georg Baselitz, Robert Motherwell, Morris Louis, Frank Stella and Magdelena Abakanowicz.

The Hess Collection

Franz Gertsch. "Johanna II" 1986. Tempera on unprimed cotton. 129⁷/₈:114¹/₄ inches.

Frank Stella. "Silverstone II" 1982. Mixed media on aluminum. 111:126:24 inches

Gilbert & George. "Flight"1983. Photo-piece 95:119 inches

Francis Bacon. "Study of Man Talking" 1981. Oil on canvas 78:58 inches

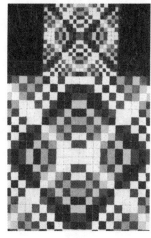

Alfred Jensen. "Sphinx of the South" 1960. Oil on canvas 72:46 inches

Leopoldo M. Maler. "Hommage" 1974. Burning typewriter. 10¹/₂:19³/₈ inches

Hidden Cellars Winery

Hidden Cellars began in the "hidden" fern grove of Mill Creek, but soon expanded and moved onto the Hildreth Ranch in Talmage. Production started at a mere 1,800 cases in 1981 and has grown to about 12,000 cases so far. Each successive vintage has been a sellout.

The winemaker, Dennis Paton, has an intimate knowledge of European wines, which he uses to to bring out the unique varietal characteristics of Mendocino County grapes, while reflecting the rich complexity of traditional European winemaking. Balanced for graceful aging, these wines may also be enjoyed when first released.

After Patton gathered some financial backing from friends, a small cabin was leased in the Ukiah area of Mendocino County, California's northernmost wine-producing region. Hard work and talent have been the hallmark of Hidden Cellars from the very beginning— and it has worked! The first crush produced a gold medal Riesling and a silver medal Zinfandel. Since that time, Hidden Cellars has collected an impressive array of medals, garnering 35 in 1990 alone.

Hidden Cellars is still growing. After being established in California, the winery expanded to the East Coast three years ago, where Hidden Cellars wines are now represented from Maine to Florida. With the recent move into the Midwest, with distribution from Illinois to Ohio, Hidden Cellars is now sold in most of the major markets around the country.

In March, 1990, Hidden Cellars released their first wine made with premium certified organically grown grapes, a Chardonnay. The fruit for this wine came from the Tillman Vineyard in Redwood Valley, in the center of Mendocino County. This late-ripening vineyard produces intense fruit flavors. The vineyard became certified by CCOF in 1982. The winemaker used only the free-run juice and light pressings for this wine. Fermentation and aging followed in French and American oak barrels. The wine was clarified, but did not go through cold stabilization.

A small addition of bisulfite (less than 50 milligrams per liter) was used to curtail browning. Patton describes this wine as "a rich, full-bodied Chardonnay redolent of succulent tropical fruit flavors, underlaid by a touch of oak." No wonder it received two gold medals in 1990, one at the Orange County Fair, and the other at the West Coast Wine Competition.

In keeping with the spirit of producing an organically grown product, recycled glass and cardboard are used to package this wine. Also, a larger than normal #10 cork (#9 is standard) has been used to reduce the risk of oxidation. Therefore, a bit more care and a little more effort is required when uncorking. The recommended storage temperature is a steady 40° to 60°F to maintain quality. Wine remaining after initial use should be resealed and refrigerated. This organically grown Chardonnay has been made to measure up to the same high standards as Hidden Cellars' other wines. The release is limited, with fewer than 250 cases in 1989.

In the spring of 1991, Hidden Cellars released its second vintage of its organically grown Chardonnay. This wine is blended from two small premium vineyards that are certified by the California Organic Foods Act of 1990 and produced in accordance with the guidelines set down by OGWA. This time they have produced around 500 cases. They have continued to barrel-ferment and age the wine "sur lie" in French and American cooperage for complexity. The winemaker describes the wine as possessing "toasty vanilla, oak aromas [in addition to] tropical fruit, lemon and banana aromas and flavors. Rich body with a lingering finish."

La Rocca Vineyards

La Rocca Vineyards is located in the Sierra Nevada mountains in northern California, about 15 miles northeast of Chico, just outside the town of Forest Ranch. The vineyard ranges from 2,300 to 2,600 feet in elevation. The soil is rich in minerals, giving it a red appearance. This is a common characteristic found in the lower Sierras, particularly in Butte County. Hot days and cool nights during the summer months coupled with the rich minerals and volcanic ash found in the soil combine to give the grapes and wines a flavor all of their own.

La Rocca Vineyards was established in 1984 with the purchase of a small, neglected 10-acre Merlot vineyard. With lots of hard work, the vineyard was reestablished and put back into production. In 1985, 60 acres of Cabernet Sauvignon grapes (located next to the Merlot) were purchased. In 1986, 80 acres of Zinfandel grapes were leased.

When Phil La Rocca took over the vineyards there was never any thought but to grow his grapes using sound organic principles. Already a commercial organic farmer (La Rocca was one of the first certified apple growers in California) and organic farm and garden instructor for more than five years, he was committed to organic grape farming immediately. Compost, rock phosphate, and lime were and still are added to the soil. Weeds are kept in check by manual and mechanical labor. Every year additional acreage is seeded with a permanent cover crop.

In 1984 La Rocca Vineyards formed a partnership with a small winery in Paradise, California, just over the ridge from Forest Ranch. An agreement was reached to process all La Rocca grapes into organic wine. No chemicals were to be used including the absolute commitment to use no sulfites in any stage of the winemaking process. From vine to bottle, all La Rocca wines are 100 percent organic. La Rocca has also sold

La Rocca Vineyards

CALIFORNIA

1986

BOTRYTIS ZINFANDEL

ALCOHOL 17% BY VOLUME

SUGAR AT TIME OF HARVEST: 32° BRIX. RESIDUAL SUGAR: 24° BRIX.

Produced & bottled by Paradise Vintners, Paradise, California.

This is a very special wine resembling the rich quality of a fine port. Because of the botrytis bacteria (The Noble Rot) each berry was hand-picked, with only the very best selected, resulting in a noble and elegant dessert wine.

From vine to bottle, the entire wine making process is completely natural using no chemicals. No sulfites were added to this wine. The result is California's purest wines.

This wine contains 100% organically grown grapes in accordance with California state regulations.

GOVERNMENT WARNING: (1) According to the Surgeon General, women should not drink alcoholic beverages during pregnancy because of the risk of birth defects. (2) Consumption of alcoholic beverages impairs your ability to drive a car or operate machinery, and may cause health problems.

The La Rocca Family

The La Roccas love horses, thus the label on their wines. They own four horses, one of which Phil rides when he works cattle for a friend, part-time. His sons and daughters have been intensely involved in horse clubs and have appeared in national competitions

grapes to other wineries around the state (some have won awards with their wines from La Rocca grapes). Certified organically grown varietals produced include Cabernet Sauvignon, Cabernet Sauvignon Blush, Merlot, Merlot Blush, Zinfandel, White Zinfandel, a botrytes White Zinfandel, a botrytes and a late harvest Zinfandel, Grenache, and French Colombard.

Butte County is now slowly gaining in reputation as a wine-growing county. Though it is an agricultural area known mostly for almonds, walnuts, prunes, and rice, Butte County was one of the first regions in California to grow wine grapes. In the late 1840s, Peter Lassen planted wine grapes; and at one time, Leland Standford had the largest wine grape vineyard in the state, which was located near the Butte–Tehana County boundary.

Las Montañas Winery

Unrefined, unfiltered, and without any chemical additives and processing are some additional qualities that distinguish Las Montañas' organically grown wines from others. Aleta Apgar, owner and winemaker, describes her unique winemaking process as "naturel," meaning the natural way. She explains, "I do not deprive them of the natural properties they need in order to continue their aging possibilities." An additional benefit is that Apgar does not add any sulfites to her wines, which is good news for those people who are sulfite-sensitive.

Located 2,000 feet up in the Mayacamas Mountains, Apgar's organic vineyards grow on Mt. Veeder. The high elevation is ideal for growing grapes, but the isolation makes it hard to find. Occasionally, visitors are invited.

The winery produces 1,000 cases of red premium wines annually, the majority of which are Zinfandel and some Cabernet Sauvignon. Apgar ages her wines in Nevres French oak barrels and tests each one before bottling. Other advantages to being a smaller producer are

Aleta Apgar and her family

63

that the wines are handcrafted (i.e., hand picked, pressed, bottled, racked, labelled, etc.) and the vineyards do not need to rely on irrigation, but are watered from naturally occurring rainfall. Also, the cool fermentation

process and premium-quality fruit produce concentrated, delicious wine. Apgar's motivation for using these methods is that the organic method does not pollute the environment, which in turn benefits our planet.

In a review in the July 31, 1989 issue of *TheWine Spectator*, her 1985 Zinfandel was described as "rich, flavorful, and flawless." Her other Cabernet and Zinfandel vintages are considered of similar quality as well.

Nevada County Wine Guild

Nevada County Wine Guild is located northwest of Lake Tahoe, which lies on the border of California and Nevada. Banner Mountain Vineyard is home of the estate-grown grapes, which make up only a small percentage of the vineyards. The remaining vineyards are located between Colfax and Nevada City, California, at an altitude above 2,500 feet.

Tony Norskog, winemaker, believes that "organic wines are not visually, nor need they be flavor-wise, different from conventionally produced wines. The salient difference is the growing technique used in the vineyard, and by some definitions (and certainly by 'eco-responsibility'), the production techniques should be at least as sensitive."

At the Nevada County Wine Guild, wines are pumped as little as possible. Most wine transfers are made by pushing the wine with inert gas pressure. The wine is made in French and American oak barrels. Often the wines are not transferred between the time of settling after

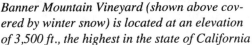
Banner Mountain Vineyard (shown above covered by winter snow) is located at an elevation of 3,500 ft., the highest in the state of California

fermentation and blending in the bottling tank. The producers do not allow people to even talk about centrifugal pumps in the wine's presence.

"Although it is easy to feel ineffective at correcting the world's problems, one can feel less impotent if in everyday life you follow a path that feels correct in your own small cosmos. This goes both for employment and consumerism," states Norskog.

All their varietal wines are produced exclusively from organically grown grapes. The transition-year grapes go into red or white table wine for local distribution. Their main varieties are Chardonnay and Pinot Noir. In 1990 they had a beautiful harvest and some very exceptional organic Zinfandel grapes were given a home at the winery as well. Two gold medals at the Orange County Fair, as well as numerous awards at local competitions, strengthen the guild's resolve that their direction is correct.

All their red wines are currently being made without sulfites. Their white wines have about 50 ppm added SO_2 at bottling for oxidative stability. This amount is approximately one-half to one-third of the usual commercial quantity, but it is a necessary addition at this time to compete with the high quality of wines with which they are presented. The SO_2 is almost entirely bound; that is, after bottling, it is no longer an antioxidant, therefore rendering the wine less objectionable to the sulfite-sensitive. Reports from sulfite-sensitive customers subtantiate no reaction to these wines.

The Nevada Country Wine Guild is the only known solar-powered winery in the United States. They are about a mile from the power grid, but it is cost-effective for them to live and operate the winery with photovoltaic power. The foothill region east of the Central Valley is ideal for organic growing. The cold winters (they have snow in the vineyard every year) and dry summers reduce insect and fungus problems. Several area vineyards (the more resistant varieties) have never had to be sprayed. The high-acid, pine forest-based soils do require an intensively managed cover crop and composting program.

So how do they taste? The 1989 Chardonnay "is one of the best organically grown wines I've tasted," writes Tom Stockley, *Seattle Times* wine columnist. He adds that it "is brimming with apple fruit, nicely balanced, and lingering in the finish. It has a very rich, appealing style (attractive label, too, with a die-cut design). . . . The 1988 Petite Sirah is a full flavored, peppery red that is also worth a try."

Octopus Mountain Cellars

Octopus Mountain Cellars exclusively produces wines made with CCOF-certified organically grown grapes from Anderson Valley in Mendocino County. This Northern California coastal valley is widely recognized as a prime viticultural region where cool Pacific breezes and a long growing season allow wine grapes to develop intense flavors and great character.

Octopus Mountain Cellars is dedicated to organic viticulture and uses modern technology while respecting traditional values to create natural wines with style and integrity. They specialize in premium varietal wines, the grapes of which are grown by the proprietors at Dennison Vineyards. This vineyard has been farmed organically since 1978 and became certified in 1983. Wine varieties include Wild Rose, White  Riesling, Vin Blanc, Chardonnay, Pinot Noir, and Cabernet Sauvignon.

According to Will Dennison, co-owner with his brother, Peter, the grapes are produced with minimal processing. The term he feels most aptly describes their farming methods is "low-input, sustainable agriculture." This encompasses applying soil amendments, such as mineral supplements, in addition to growing cover crops such as legumes to enrich the soil and add organic matter. "We strive to produce grapes that will make the highest quality wine," he adds. "Organic farming techniques are a key factor in this process."

Octopus Mountain Cellars produces sound, healthy wines that are free from flaws and defects. Their goal is to make wines that are fresh and fruity with distinctive qualities, wines that are a pure expression of the grape, the vineyard, and the vintage. Octopus Mountain wines can be appreciated for their delicate balance and youthful exuberance and will age gracefully to evolve further in the bottle.

Olson Winery

Located in the Redwood Valley of Mendocino County, Olson Winery produces 9,000 cases of wine yearly, the grapes of which are grown in accordance with California's organic certification standards. No sulfur dioxide is used at any time during the fermentation process. Only at bottling are minimal amounts used to preserve the quality of the wine and prevent bottle variation.

John Eppler, winery manager, states that grapes can be organically farmed almost as easily and sometimes more economically than commercially farmed ones. He adds that the less the wine is processed, the more fruit and flavors are preserved in the wines, yielding a better quality.

Organically grown varieties include Zinfandel, Merlot and Cabernet Sauvignon. They also produce some award-winning transitional wines as well. In a wine tasting by eight *Longevity* magazine staffers, Olson's Fumé Blanc, 1986, was described as one of the best compared with several other organic wines from California, New York, and France. They described it as "a perfect summer wine—lively, easy drinking and tastes best well chilled." In addition, their 1987 Zinfandel won a gold medal and their 1986 Cabernet Sauvignon a silver medal.

Orleans Hill Winery

Orleans Hill has been producing award-winning wines for 10 years and presently produces as many as 6,000 cases of wine annually. Their small operation allows them to spend time interacting, monitoring, and perfecting their wines. Jim Lapsley, winemaker, realizes the neccessity of being committed to the preservation of the planet. His personal interest reflects that belief. Lapsley owns his own organic garden and is active with OGWA. He recognized that he had a fantastic opportunity to bring his beliefs into actuality by producing wine in its most ancient and purest form, while balancing this simplicity with the modern technological powers of sanitary storage and filtration. Lapsley states, "this CCOF-certified organically grown wine is designed to be as competitive and pleasing as its more chemically manipulated brethren."

The result of their efforts is their Organic Red Zinfandel Nouveau. This labor-intensive wine is produced through a "whole-cluster" fermentation, which allows the grapes to ferment their juice within the full berries. This method provides a greater extraction of flavors such as blackberry, as well as a deep rich color. The wine is bottled with some residual carbon dioxide and has an intense fruity character. Within the bottle, the wine becomes stabilized. It is recommended that for a full experience of this wine, it is best to taste it at various intervals after opening. The reason is that there is a definite budding of aroma, complexity, and fruity flavor, plus a slight tingle from the residual gas that will continue to protect the wine from oxidation.

Lapsley comments that it is not appropriate to compare this wine with more complex, aged Zinfandel or Cabernet varieties, or even Gamay Beaujolais. "This wine is targeted for immediate consumption, easy enjoyment, and purity of product," he explains. Its uniqueness does not come from its manipulation, but its powerful expression of non-aged Zinfandel juice.

The *San Francisco Chronicle* stated that the 1990 harvest was perfect in California for the production of nouveau wines. Grapes ripened evenly over the entire month of September under dry, warm conditions. The Orleans Hill Zinfandel was recommended and was described as possessing "a wonderful rush of intense blackberry aromas on the nose. On the palate, the wine is like fresh grapes and plums, a lovely wine." No wonder it won a prestigious bronze medal at the Intervin International Wine Competition and a gold medal at the California State Fair. In November 1991, Orleans Hill released a Sauvignon Blanc and White Zinfandel. Both contain fewer than 15 ppm added sulfites.

Like most nouveaux, Orleans Hill's Zinfandel is best consumed by mid-spring, when the deep perfume of the wine is at its best. If it is stored in a cool environment, nouveau wines will keep for one to two years, but there will be some loss in fruit flavors.

Paul Thomas Winery

Paul Thomas Winery is located in Bellevue, Washington, where ten different wine types are produced. Established in August 1979 by Paul Thomas, the winery has an established reputation for producing many of the highest quality wines available from Washington. Paul Thomas is a social activist and former high school history and economics teacher, and his wife, Judy, an artist. The winery began as a producer of dry-style fruit wines made from rhubarb, bing cherry, raspberry, and Bartlett pear. It now produces a full range of award-winning grape wines in addition to the original fruit wines.

Their Crimson Rhubarb wine is made from rhubarb that is organically grown in Puyallup, Washington. It is a lovely pale pink and, contrary to most expectations, is finished as a dry wine. In the Northwest, it is one of their top-selling products. The newsletter of the Puget Consumers' Co-op, a health food cooperative in Seattle, states that, "The exciting thing about Paul's wines . . . is the concern Paul has for the

WASHINGTON

CRIMSON RHUBARB
WINE

ALC. 12% BY VOL.

Paul Thomas

CRIMSON RHUBARB
WINE

Made from rhubarb organically grown in
Washington State's Puyallup Valley, this
dry wine is delightful with broiled salmon,
barbecue fare, and by itself. Serve chilled.

PRODUCED AND BOTTLED BY PAUL THOMAS, BELLEVUE, WA
BOTTLING DATE MARCH, 1990

GOVERNMENT WARNING: (1)
ACCORDING TO THE SURGEON GEN-
ERAL WOMEN SHOULD NOT DRINK
ALCOHOLIC BEVERAGES DURING
PREGNANCY BECAUSE OF THE RISK
OF BIRTH DEFECTS. (2) CONSUMP-
TION OF ALCOHOLIC BEVERAGES IM-
PAIRS YOUR ABILITY TO DRIVE A CAR
OR OPERATE MACHINERY, AND MAY
CAUSE HEALTH PROBLEMS.

purity and quality of the ingredients he uses. Of special interest to many Co-op members is the fact that Paul strives to get organically grown or unsprayed fruit whenever possible" (*PCC Sound Consumer*, 1987). Their rhubarb has been purchased from the same organic grower for years.

This wine contains no detected sulfites and is carried by several healthfood stores. In fact, the Products Compliance Division of the Bureau of Alcohol, Tobacco, and Firearms (BATF) of the U.S. Treasury Department granted permission to exclude the designation, "CONTAINS SULFITES," on their wine label. Apparently, rhubarb, as compared with grapes, does not produce detectable sulfites (fewer than 10 ppm) during fermentation.

Because fruit for winemaking needs a sugar content of about 20 to 22 percent to ferment properly, Thomas has to add some sugar to most of his fruit wines, especially the rhubarb, which has a natural sugar content of only 4 percent. During the fermentation process, all the sugar is converted to alcohol.

Paul Vineyards

Paul Vineyards, producer of organic wine grapes, is located about 150 miles north of San Francisco and about 40 miles from the ocean. The crop for 1990 was good, quality-wise, but tonnage was way down. While the grapes were in bloom, they had an unusual 6 inches of rain the last week of May and the first week of June 1990. The flowers were damaged by the rain so many of the vines did not finish the flowering cycle. The grapes that did develop, though, were of the highest quality. They have been growing grapes since 1950 and have never used sprays or pesticides of any kind. For more than 30 years, they have been farming with methods similar to organic. The grapes are sold to a commercial wine producer who blends them with its own commercial grapes to achieve balance.

Elizabeth Paul states that their main motivation for growing grapes organically was the inspiration of their old neighbor who came from Italy in 1906. He planted his vineyard in 1928 and it is still producing today. He said that a vine needs five things: pruning, suckering, cultivating the soil, a dusting with sulfur, and rain. In addition, "a love of the

The Paul Family

land and believing in what you're producing" is what Paul believes farming is all about. She expressed excitement about her involvement with OGWA when they adopted the French organic wine standards. When asked about fertilizers, Paul said that they basically dry farm and use cover crops and apply mushroom compost when the vines are planted.

Ponderosa Vineyards

Ponderosa Vineyards is operated by the Looney family, owners and operators of the first winery in Linn County, Oregon. Some of their children (six sons, one daughter) help with harvesting, bottling, and operating the winery. In 1843, the first Looney family traveled across the Rocky Mountains on the Applegate wagon train to settle in the Willamette Valley. There, the Looneys built a farm and they have remained in the valley ever since. Ponderosa Vineyards' wine labels symbolize their family heritage. The pine trees represent the Ponderosa pines on the property, and the covered wagon represents the family's journey across the Rocky Mountains. Each figure in the covered wagon scene portrays a member of the family when the winery first opened.

Bill Looney and his sons planted the initial vineyard in 1978 and built their first winery in 1979.

The Looney Family

71

Because of the soil conditions and lack of irrigation, it was not until 1987 before they harvested their first grape crop, producing 850 gallons of wine. The next year they had a better crop, which produced 1,100 gallons. Their landmark year was 1988, when they sold their first three bottles of wine. Hard work and perseverance finally paid off in 1990, when their Pinot Noir received a bronze medal at the Oregon State Fair in competition against 47 other wines. The following year, their 1991 Red Table Wine received a silver medal at the Oregon State Fair in competition against 56 other wines.

Ponderosa Vineyards' wines are totally natural; nothing is added. Because the Looneys believe that some people who experience headaches, shortness of breath, and other discomforts are suffering the effects of drinking wines with preservatives, they decided to be the first winery in Oregon to produce wine with no added sulfites or preservatives. They are expected to complete Oregon state's four-year requirements for the "certified organically grown" designation in 1992.

Ponderosa Vineyards presently produces five transitional wines: Pinot Noir, dry Vin Rosé, Red Table Wine, and several sweet wines—Semi-Sweet Aperitif–Satisfaction Plus, and Dessert Wine. Their Pinot Noir is "a dry, mellow and full-bodied wine with an oak and berry flavor." Semi-Sweet Aperitif–Satisfaction Plus is a fruity, semi-sweet wine made from Sauvignon Blanc with a touch of brandy. After the bottle has been opened, the wine may last up to two months if refrigerated. Their Dessert Wine also has a touch of brandy in it, and it holds the same as Semi-Sweet Aperitif. It can be described as "sweet, rich and creamy." Both of their sweet wines have an alcohol content of 18 percent because of the added brandy. This allows them to forgo the use of sulfites. People who like both sweet and dry wines will particularly enjoy the Semi-Sweet Apertif–Satisfaction Plus.

Because their wine is still alive, it may produce a small amount of sediment; when this occurs, the Looneys recommend decanting. To maintain their wines, they suggest storing them as you would any other high-quality wine. They also recommend using a wine saver, which can be found in almost any wine specialty shop. Properly used, a wine saver removes the oxygen from the top of the wine, allowing the wine to hold longer. They have found that this allows an opened bottle to stay fresh much longer.

Prager Winery and Port Works

Prager Winery and Port Works in Napa Valley is a special example of a small family winery. They produce 3,600 cases a year and are at full capacity because of the demand of Prager Ports and the joint efforts of Jim Prager's three sons.

The Pragers were not born into winemaking, but owning and operating a small winery in Napa Valley was a burning ambition of the family patriarch, and former Southern California insurance executive, Jim Prager. With the support of his wife, Imogene, Prager walked away from a successful career and all the urban security and comforts that went with it. They moved with their seven children, all still in school, to sunny St. Helena. In 1980, the first year of production, port wines were the first to be made. Thus the term "Port Works" was developed. Port takes time to make; to keep the winery going the first few years, Prager and his sons worked at neighboring wineries until their wines were available for sale.

Prager's philosophy of winemaking goes back to the Old World style. He states that, "There is not the 'standard' modern style of winemaking here. . . . Prager Winery is producing wines and ports as they used to be produced for hundreds of years prior to the advent of electricity and high tech. This style of wine tastes better and ages (lasts) longer in the bottle." In the vineyards, no pesticides or chemical fertilizers of any kind are used, nor is the vineyard irrigated. Prager practices dry farming (no irrigation). No chemicals are used in his winemaking either, to produce a truly natural wine. The red wines and the ports are fermented using the native yeasts on the grapes, and they contain no added sulfites. Prager Winery is one of the few that can print the statement "NO SULFITES ADDED" on its labels. The natural sulfite content is so small (1–12 ppm) that the government does not even require any mention, but Prager fully discloses the ppm content on his labels.

All the Prager ports have roughly half or less the sweetness level of other California ports, which attracts attention to other flavors and complexities in the wine, according to Prager. Their Noble Companion

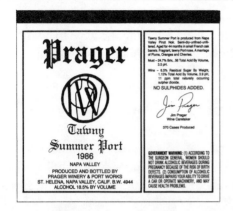

Port is made from Cabernet Sauvignon, their Royal Escort Port from Petite Sirah, and their Tawny Summer Port from Pinot Noir grapes. Prager contends that these wines can be enjoyed for these nuances of flavor, not just for the sweetness.

Prager not only specializes in ports, but produces small amounts of table wine: Zinfandel, Chardonnay, and Cabernet Sauvignon. Table wines account for 25 percent of their current production. Their whites contain less than 10 ppm sulfites. No sulfites are added at any time.

A visit to this small winery will guarantee the opportunity to talk wine with the owner, or with one of his three sons, Jeff, Peter, or John. Jeff is the general manager as well as the artist who designs the labels and logo for the winery. Peter studied at Fresno State and graduated in 1991 with a degree in enology (science of winemaking). In 1987, John took over the position of cellarmaster, and since then production has gradually increased with his

knowledge and care. Occasionally, you may find Imogene in the tasting room, but most likely she will be on the phone taking care of business for her successful Prager Winery Bed and Breakfast.

San Pietro Vara Vineyard and Wine Company

San Pietro Vara Vineyard and Wine Company was established in 1979. Grapes from this vineyard, located at the head of the Napa Valley, north of Calistoga, were sold to premium wineries in the area until 1983. That year, the owners of San Pietro Vara, Albert and Norma Giordano and Les and Lil Widman, decided to crush their own grapes and produce premium estate-bottled wines.

When asked about their definition of what distinguishes an organic wine, Norma Giordano replied that it is "a wine that you know has been made sensibly from natural elements [and] allowed to develop and mature without being forced or stimulated by additives of any kind." In addition, the vineyard is not irrigated and organic methods and cultural practices are used exclusively. No herbicides, pesticides, or synthetic fertilizers are used. As of 1990, San Pietro Vara was the first and the only Napa Valley vineyard to be certified by CCOF. Four varieties of black grapes contribute to the major portion of their wine production: Merlot, Cabernet Sauvignon, Zinfandel, and Charbono. From time to time, quality grapes, such as the 1986 Gamay, can be purchased from other Napa Valley vineyards to produce varietals that San Pietro Vara does not produce itself.

When asked about their motivation for using organic over commercial techniques, Norma Giordano replied, "Our winemaker, Al Giordano, a child of the '30s, grew up in an era when the use of insecticides and pesticides was not prevalent. At that time, small farmers used semiorganic methods of farming; that is, whatever manure or waste crop that was available was utilized to help improve the soil. In some cases, small amounts of commercial fertilizers were used. It occurred to us that small farms today using these older methods should be able to prosper as did the farmers of that era. Another motivation was economic. Our own labor used in cultivation practices is far less expensive than buying commercial fertilizers or pesticides. In addition, we just didn't like the idea of handling the hazardous commercial products."

Family at work in the winery

From left to right: John Silver (friend), Ron Dixon (cousin), Anthony Giordano (uncle), Albert Giordano, Lil Widman (Al's aunt and partner), Les Widman (uncle and partner)

The winery crushed its first grapes in 1983 and had its first release in 1988, the medal-winning 1983 Charbono. The certified organically grown wines produced by San Pietro Vara contain no chemical additives of any kind. Natural yeasts are allowed to ferment but are sometimes supplemented by cultured yeasts to ensure that fermentation is completed. The natural yeasts add complexity not normally found in commercial wines. Sulfites are quite low and are naturally occurring or are a product of the fermentation process. No sulfites have been added. In addition, none of the wines has been fined or filtered. Bottling time is determined by taste, not by the calendar. And no wines have been bottled under three years of age. Racking is done frequently to eliminate the need for fining or filtering.

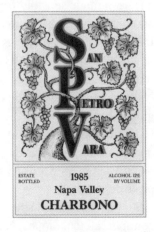

Current capacity of the winery is approximately 3,000 cases per year. Plans are to grow very slowly to ensure that the highest quality will be maintained.

Recent releases include their 1984 Estate Zinfandel, 1985 Estate Charbono, and a fine 1986 Napa Valley Gamay wine. Future releases will be their estate-bottled Merlot and Cabernet Sauvignon. San Pietro Vara wines can be found in fine restaurants and selected wine shops and natural food stores in the San Francisco Bay Area, California.

Silver Thread Vineyard

With its premiere vintage in 1991, Silver Thread Vineyard is the first organic vineyard and winery in the eastern United States specializing in the classic European varieties. The vineyard was established in 1982 on the east shore of Seneca Lake, in the heart of New York's Finger Lakes district. The microclimate created by Seneca Lake, the deepest and warmest of the Finger Lakes, has proved very favorable for the grapes that make the best wines of northern France and Germany.

Silver Thread Vineyard has never used herbicides or insecticides and has followed the certification guidelines of the Natural Organic Farmers Association of New York since 1988. Three estate-bottled organically grown wines are produced: barrel-fermented Chardonnay, an off-dry Riesling, and Pinot Noir. A sparkling wine that blends Pinot Noir and Chardonnay is also planned. The wines are made with minimal disruption of the lakeside ecosystem and minimal intervention in the wine cellar to capture the purest imprint of each year upon their piece of land.

Topolos at Russian River Vineyards

Russian River Vineyards, founded in 1963, dominates the horizon in Forestville, in west Sonoma County. The architecture of Topolos Winery is influenced by hop kilns and Russian architecture at Fort Ross. Its rustic charm emanates the history and quality of Sonoma County wine production.

The winery houses more than 200 French oak barrels filled with premium certified organically grown wine, assorted stainless steel storage and fermenting tanks, and a small 7,500-case family winery that is devoted to producing gold-medal, environment-friendly wines.

A 114-year-old manor house at the winery serves as the showplace restaurant, known in the county for the finest in outdoor dining, delicious food, and a cordial staff. The garden entrance is a marvelous capsule of several varieties of drought-tolerant native plant species found in Sonoma County.

Topolos strives for varietal distinction and high extract, color, aroma, and flavor in their wines. "We make wine for the true wine lover, not the faint of heart." They dry farm and organically grow their total production of grapes. This includes planting legumes in the fall for green manure, harboring beneficials, and using responsible application of elemental sulfur during the growing season. They use no synthetic pesticides, herbicides, or fungicides. In addition, Topolos uses the Vaslin press from France. It is a very old press, but is gentle, giving the top-quality pressing that they strive for. Their goal is to build, not deplete, the soil. "We feel that dirt has a bad name. Our friend, dirt, is the foundation of our winery. We respect its components and it returns to us bounty that is clean and delicious."

Topolos produces Chardonnay, Sauvignon Blanc, Zinfandel, Petite Sirah, Alicante-Bouschet and Grand Noir, a Rhône-style red. Several of these have received gold medals. Their wines are now available

Topolos is one of only four restaurant and winery combinations in Sonoma County, and it is the only one that is family-run. The charming and intimate rooms, patio and gardens can accomodate up to 200 guests for Sunday brunches, luncheons, dinners, and catered events. Summer weddings are especially popular

in Arizona, California, Washington, Colorado, North Carolina, New York, New Jersey, Connecticut, Florida, and Quebec, Canada.

In addition to having their wines certified by CCOF, Topolos is a member of OGWA and works within their parameters for clean wine production; they add no more than 25 ppm sulfur at bottling.

Their awards and favorable wine reviews are numerous. The *Underground Wine Journal, A Definitive Guide to the Finest Wines of the World*, named their 1988 Sonoma County Zinfandel a "Best Buy." According to the journal, "there is a blackberry-like fruit on the perfumed nose of this medium ruby wine with hints of spice, currants and pepper. There are berry and black currant flavors on the palate with tinges of pepper and cherry. It is complex, well-balanced, has good depth, balanced acidity and a moderately long, lingering finish. . . ." Jerry Mead, publisher of *The Wine Trader* in San Francisco, describes their 1986 Petite Sirah as possessing "flavors of black cherry and chocolate . . . [the] body and texture are extractive and chewy." The 1985 vintage won the only gold in its class at the Sonoma Harvest Fair, and their 1987 a gold medal at the Wine Guild International Wine Tasting at Fort Lauderdale, Florida. Another prize was their 1986 Sonoma Alicante-Bouschet. It is "a collector's item in the making," says Mead. It won a gold medal at the 1988 Orange County Fair and is one of the only two wines still made from this variety in California. In addition, it is one of only a few grapes in the world to have red juice as well as red skin, so expect very deep color extraction. Their 1987 Rossi Ranch Zinfandel won a gold medal at the Eighth Annual West Coast Wine Competition at Reno, Nevada. And their 1988 vintage was selected as wine of the month in the *Grape Press*. They described it as posessing "rich

garnet color, and medium depth [which] enhances fresh red raspberries with lively acid. Aging in French oak barrels added structure as well as a light oak flavor. This classic Zinfandel with good tannin balance is drinkable now, but will age well for several years to come."

If you would like information on how to obtain any of the wines mentioned in this book, contact: The Organic Connection, Post Office Box 88, Tempe, Arizona 85280, telephone (602) 894-2997.

CLASSIFICATION OF U.S. ORGANIC WINERIES

These classifications of U.S. wine producers represent growing methods only. Some of the wineries produce wines by commercial means as well. The classifications are defined in the preceding chapter. The page numbers in the right-hand column indicate where you can find a description of the wine producer's location, motivation for farming organically, and special techniques used.

KEY: *OG = organically grown; COG = certified organically grown;*
      T = transitional; < = less than

U.S. Producers	Classifi- cation	Sulfites added (ppm)	Page
Amity Vineyards	COG	None	42
Badger Mountain Vineyard and Winery	COG	< 50	43
Bellerose Vineyard	OG	<100	44
Blue Heron Lake Winery	T	<100	46
Briceland Vineyards	OG/COG	< 30	47
Cameron Winery	COG	None	48
H. Coturri and Sons	OG	None	49
Fetzer Vineyards	COG	<100	50
Fitzpatrick Winery	COG	<100	52
Frey Vineyards	COG	None	53
Hallcrest Vineyards/Organic Wine Works	OG/COG	<100/None	55
Hess Collection Winery	T	<100	57
Hidden Cellars Winery	COG	<100	60
La Rocca Vineyards	OG	None	61
Las Montañas Winery	OG	None	63
Nevada County Wine Guild	OG	None/<50	64
Octopus Mountain Cellars	COG	<100	66
Olson Winery	OG/T	<100	67
Orleans Hill Winery	COG	None	68
Paul Thomas Winery	OG	None	69
Ponderosa Vineyards	T	None	71
Prager Winery and Port Works	OG	None/<30	73
San Pietro Vara Vineyard and Wine Company	COG	None	74
Silver Thread Vineyard	OG	<100	76
Topolos at Russian River Vineyards	COG	< 25	77

Importers and Distributors of Organic Wines

This section presents information submitted by French, German, and Italian organic wine importers and distributors regarding their interest in carrying organic wine. Included is a brief introduction of the organic wineries they represent and a description of the wines available for wholesale in the United States. Several of them distribute domestic organic wines as well. As you will discover, the following information can be a valuable tool for selecting a wine. The subject index can also benefit readers who would like information regarding a particular wine or winery.

Chartrand Imports

Chartrand Imports began importing organic French wines to the United States in 1985. They were the first company to import and sell a line of organic wines in this country. Paul Chartrand worked in the natural foods and organic farming field with the Maine Organic Farmers and Gardeners Association before entering the importing business. He discovered wonderful wines made by organic growers in France during a trip in 1982 and spent several months as an apprentice in organic vineyards before returning with the idea of making these wines available to health- and quality-conscious wine lovers. He has spent the past eight years establishing relationships with France's best organic vineyards.

Chartrand Imports sells only wines that are certified organic by independent third-party verification (i.e., the label includes the Nature et Progrès seal of approval). In France there are three such organizations, all with basically the same standards (see p.15).

Chartrand provides wines from fifteen individual organic vineyards that represent all the major wine regions of France. Château Méric produces two complex and full-flavored wines, a red and a white from the Graves region of Bordeaux. One tasting panel found their red to be "the best of the bunch — heady scent, smooth, full, rich taste." They have been certified by Nature et Progrès since the organization was founded in the early 1960s. The vineyard is encompassed by forests, protecting it from pollution. Château Moulin de Peyronin makes a very pleasant light-bodied red Bordeaux. The Jougla family, owners of this 24-acre estate, follows all French organic requirements and has been growing the vineyards since 1966 without any chemical treatment.

The white Entre-Deux-Mers from Domaine du Bourdieu is a simple, fruity summer pleaser. The Domaine has grown grapes organically since 1963 and all wines are certified by the National Federation of Organic Agriculture. The Domaine also produces white and red Bordeaux under the name Domaine Ste. Anne, as well as a sparkling wine labeled Le Bourdieu. All Bordeaux wines use Cabernet Sauvignon and Merlot in the reds, and Sauvignon Blanc and Sémillon in the whites.

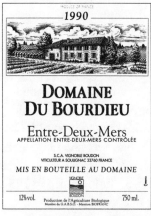

Guy Chaumont's 1986 Bourgogne Pinot Noir is a velvety, berrylike red wine. His Bourgogne Chardonnay is a buttery, oak-aged white wine that is drier than most American Chardonnays. Both wines have fruity bouquets and full, smooth flavors. The Chaumont Vineyard was converted to organic growing methods more than twenty years ago and has been certified by Nature et Progrès. The 1986 Pinot Noir has no detectable sulfites and says so on the label.

From further north in the Burgundy region come several rare and delicious red and white wines, made from Pinot Noir or Chardonnay, respectively. The André Chaumont family produces a very hearty and full-bodied Mercurey red wine that is a pleasant accompaniment to meat dishes. Jean-Claude and Pierrette Rateau practice biodynamic agriculture. From their Clos des Mariages vineyard they make a red Beaune that is delicate and full of the ripe fruit flavors of Pinot Noir. They also make a small amount of famous Puligny-Montrachet white from the Corvée des Vignes vineyard. This rich and long-lasting Chardonnay is a wine to savor. Jean Javillier is a producer of another famous white Burgundy in the town of Meursault, for which the wine is named. Another delicious white is the Côte de Beaune from Emmanuel Giboulot, who makes this wine from very old Chardonnay vines that are not often used in this appellation. It has a pleasing melon-like taste that is accented by oak aging. All the vineyards are certified organic; Javillier, Giboulot, and Rateau are all associated with Nature et Progrès, and Chaumont is certified by U.N.I.A. (the National Interprofessional Union of Agrobiologists).

Southern France's organic wines include Domaine Terres Blanches, Château Bousquette, and Domaine des Cedres, who produce tasty red wine blends of Grenache, Syrah, and several lesser known varieties, as is common in the area. Their spicy, peppery, and well-rounded flavors make them

excellent wines for pasta, casseroles, and any other

Mediterranean-style cooking, as well as for backyard barbecues, American style. A pleasing white wine from the South is Domaine de Petit Roubié's Picpoul de Pinet, with a light nose of nuts and fruit, and a dry finish for summer enter-

taining. Domaine Terres Blanches is certified by Terre et Vie, Château Bousquette and Domaine de Petit Roubié by Nature et Progrès, and Domaine des Cedres by the National Federation of Organic Agriculture.

In the north of France, the climate favors the white and sparkling wines that Chartrand imports. In the Loire Valley, Guy Bossard produces a dry, citrus-tinged wine called Muscadet de Sèvre-et-Maine. It

is perfect for seafood and picnics. His méthode champenoise is a light, fruity sparkling version of the same wine. He has been certified by Terre et Vie since 1974. Serge Faust makes his champagnes in the region that gives its name to these world-famous sparkling wines. These wines have

a rich, yeasty fruit flavor and a dry finish to bring you back for more. They are made from a blend of Pinot Meunier, Pinot Noir, and Chardonnay grapes. André Stentz produces Riesling and Gewürztraminer wines in Alsace, the most eastern of France's wine regions. These are very aromatic and richly flavored whites that can accompany a variety of dishes and also serve as pleasant apertifs. His vineyard is certified by Nature et Progrès.

From across the German border, Chartrand imports a white Müller-Thurgau wine and a red Pinot Noir, or Spätburgunder, from Jorg Scheel's Sonnenbrunnen Winery near Freiburg, which is certified organic by the Federal Association of Organic Viticulture.

Washington Times wine columnist William Clifford named the 1990 Müller-Thurgau "Wine of the Week." Sonnenbrunnen, founded in 1984, also produces organically grown sparkling wine, schnapps, and fruit brandies, in addition to other wine varieties. Chartrand Imports offers several wines with no added sulfur that are available in addition to their full line of organic wines.

Chartrand Imports currently offers 24 organic wines and is constantly adding new ones as the distribution widens. Chartrand also hopes to offer several Italian organic wines. Distributors sell Chartrand Imports' wines in Arizona, New England, New York, Maryland, Ohio, Pennsylvania, California, Michigan, Texas, and Washington, D.C.

Kermit Lynch Wine Merchants

Kermit Lynch has been importing French and Italian wines for two decades. He is the author of *Adventures on the Wine Route, A Wine Buyer's Tour of France*. The book explains Lynch's passion for natural, living wine. He writes,

> "Organic" is a word that does not work in a wine shop. The word seems to have a negative impact on most wine connoisseurs. And it is true that many organically produced wines are liable to fizz, gurgle, and stink to high heaven because no chemicals have been used to kill possible yeasts and bacteria.
>
> However, there is another side to the question. Even if I were a health nut, but I am not. Still, I look very closely at organically produced wines when I hear of them because what you have is the unadulterated product of earth, vine, and man. Man's part of the equation, the vinification, can be well or poorly executed, but if we find a winemaker of talent who knows how to bottle a clean wine, then an organic wine has a good chance to be interesting. Once you start throwing chemical fertilizers into the soil to increase production, chemical treatments onto the vines to kill pests, and yet others into the wine itself to stabilize it, you change the quality and personality of what comes out through the vine into the grape and ultimately into your wineglass. That fundamental expression of soil and fruit is distorted. Chemicals increase production, they may protect the wine from nature's quirks, but they also muck up the elemental statement that wine is capable of making. (pp. 164–165)

Lynch sells several organically produced wines, some of which have become world famous and fetch high prices; others are little known and remarkably inexpensive.

From Italy is Steffano Bellotti. As a young man who was diagnosed as having cancer, Bellotti left the big city, moved to a little farm, and devoted himself to organic grape growing and wine production. His white Gavi is aged in large casks made from acacia wood. No other Gavi possesses such style and personality. It is certified by Nature et Progrès.

Domaine du Bas Deffens is a Coteaux Varois country red from Provence. It is rustic, hearty, and flavorful. It is certified by Nature et Progrès.

Domaine de la Jasse is located in Violes near Gigondas in the Côtes-du-Rhône region. The soil is extremely stony, exactly like the soil at Châteauneuf-du-Pape. The vinification is old-fashioned, producing a big,

aromatic wine with great complexity, which resembles a fine Châteauneuf-du-Pape. This wine is certified by Nature et Progrès.

No region of France has suffered more from chemical pesticides, herbicides, and fertilizers than the Beaujolais. Christian Ducroux was scorned when he began to practice organic farming methods. Today, a handful of neighbors drop in or call to ask his advice. He makes a Beaujolais nouveau, which Lynch ships by plane each year, and a grand cru Beaujolais Régnié, certified by Nature et Progrès.

The grand cru Morgon from Marcel Lapierre is also organically produced. Each year Lynch selects a few barrels that are not only unfiltered, but have no sulfur dioxide added. The aroma is wild and meaty, loaded with fruit and flavor.

Lynch's least expensive red is a vin de pays (country wine) rouge from the Domaine de la Gautière. A chapter of Lynch's book is devoted to Gautière. The

wine is a blend of Syrah, Grenache, and Cinsault and certified by Nature et Progrès.

The most talked about young winery in the world is the Domaine du Daumas Gassac in the Languedoc region of southern France. The French magazine *Gault-Millau* called it "the Lafite of the Languedoc." The *Times* of London said Daumas Gassac's red is "actually more like Latour than Lafite with its enormous color and immense, hefty, tannic character." The wine is produced primarily from Cabernet grapes. A small bit of dry white is also produced—expensive, but an altogether remarkable wine.

Domaine de Trévallon produces a Syrah–Cabernet Sauvignon blend. The grapes are organically grown in the rockiest vineyard in Provence, France. The jagged chunks of rock look like they would be more at home on the Moon. The wine is rich, ample, and heady, and it ages beautifully. Wine connoisseur Robert Parker, Jr., states, "One of the greatest discoveries in my life has been the wine made at the Domaine de Trévallon."

Kermit Lynch protects his treasures. They are shipped in temperature-controlled containers and stored in his air-conditioned warehouse.

Natural Wines Internationale

Natural Wines Internationale began organizing its resources in late 1990 to supply the rapidly growing demand for delicious, environment-friendly, organic wine. The founders had learned about the availability of organic wine because of their interest in health and enhancing life on this planet. They were impressed that most of the wineries were using minimal or no sulfites, certified organically grown grapes, and natural processing methods, and that the wines were of equal or greater quality and taste compared with commercial wines. As a result of these positive factors, the founders wanted to support the other new organic businesses arising in the United States. They were not only professionals in specialized careers, but began to view themselves as inspired pioneers, "environmental ambassadors" to help save our planet and improve people's lives. This motivation is embodied in the name "natural," which in Latin (naturel) refers to "nature at its fullest," hence Natural Wines Internationale.

They anticipate providing at least 50 of the highest quality "Select" organic wines from producers in California, Oregon, Washington, France, Germany, and Italy. In fact, many of the wines described in this book, and more, are available through their marketing efforts.

Their commitment to using refrigerated transportation and air-conditioned storage assures their customers that their organic wines will be delivered from producer to consumer with the ecology intact that makes wine so health-enhancing and delicious. With Natural Wines Internationale, you are assured the highest quality product, educational support, product literature, and competitive service.

Organic Vintages

Steve Frenkel founded Organic Vintages in 1988 to help provide an alternative for the Earth- and health-conscious consumer, and to demonstrate that quality grapes can be grown and processed without synthetic applications. He has been a long-term supporter of sustainable agriculture and encourages the transition to organic viticulture by all grape growers. Organic Vintages is a licensed importer and distributor of fine organic wines, champagnes, and sake, representing more than 25 producers from France, Italy, Japan, Germany and the United States. They are currently the largest distributor of organic wines in New York, now serving more than 250 retail shops and restaurants. They are also wholesalers in California and New Jersey and soon will make their products available in many other states.

Among their French line are Château la Maubastit, Domaine de Tavernel, Berjerac, and Gerard Leroux. Château la Maubastit is from Bordeaux, a region well known for its high-quality wine grapes.

Maubastit has been producing certified organic wines since 1980. Their red wine is made from 50 percent Merlot, 20 percent Cabernet Sauvignon, and 30 percent Cabernet Franc. At the 1991 Natural Foods Expo East held in Baltimore, Maryland, comments about the wine ranged from "smooth with considerable depth" to "elegant and well developed." From Gironde, France comes

Domaine de Tavernel, a family-owned winery for more than 70 years. They have been certified organic since 1985. Tavernel produces a red table wine called la

Sarabande, made from 80 percent Carignane and 20 percent Cabernet Sauvignon. It can be described as "a

country-styled medium-bodied wine with cherry and spice overtones and a smooth lingering finish . . . an enjoyable casual sipper." Château la Maubastit, Domaine de Tavernel, and Berjerac are all certified by the European Federation of Agrobiology Syndicate (F.E.S.A.), which is the same as Terre et Vie.

Gerard Leroux is another organic viticulturalist who has produced an impressive array of fine organic wines: Saumur, a vintage méthode champenoise sparkling wine, Coteaux du Layon, a Cabernet Sauvignon labeled Anjou, and two rosés—Rosé de Loire and Rosé d'Anjou. All are certified organic by

Nature et Progrès and have received the special designation Appellation
Contrôlée, France's top category.

Among their Italian line is La
Suvera, producer of Demeter-certified
biodynamically grown white table
wine and an estate-bottled red table
wine called Rango Rosso. La Suvera
is certified by The Demeter
Association.

Organic Vintages also
imports several organic sakes from
Japan—Mitoku Organic Brown Rice
Sake, Organic White Rice Sake, and Mikawa Organic Sweet Rice
Brandy—in addition to providing a wide variety of domestic wines.

Organic Wine Company

Based in San Francisco, the Organic Wine Company was founded by
Veronique Raskin. A native of France who came to San Francisco
originally to establish a psychology practice, Raskin learned of organic
wine in 1977 after her grandfather started growing grapes organically on
the family estate, Domaine de la Bousquette. This 50-acre estate is
located in southern France and has been in her family since the French
Revolution.

Discovering that she could enjoy the wines her grandfather
made without experiencing headaches that often accompanied
commercial wines, and realizing that others could benefit from her
discovery, in 1980 she began distributing wines in the United States. In

1983, Domaine de la Bosquette became the first imported wine on the U.S. market with "organic" on the label. In recent years she has expanded the firm's catalog to include more than a dozen organic reds, whites, and rosés. "We've made it possible for American consumers to choose certified organic wines without sacrificing quality or selection," states Ms. Raskin. The company sells only Appellation Contrôlée wines from several regions. Wine drinkers can enjoy a rich Côtes du Rhône, a lively Bordeaux Blanc, and even

a méthode champenoise sparkling wine, each produced to the highest organic standards. Already, the Organic Wine Company's wines can be found across the country—Arizona, California, Oregon, Colorado, Illinois, Iowa, Minnesota, Washington, and Wisconsin.

Raskin feels strongly about the poisons that are put into the Earth, and the goal of the Organic Wine Company is not only to import the finest organic French wines available, but to make people aware of ecological concerns as well. Her grandfather initiated her zeal with his commonsense value system: even though he was an old man, he was still concerned about how his farming practices would effect future generations. Raskin carries on his tradition by offering environmentally responsible wines that do not compromise quality.

For 10 years, the Organic Wine Company's goal has been, and will continue to be, to attract the attention of wine drinkers and enlist them as "environmental ambassadors" to eventually turn around the current worldwide destructive agricultural practices. The battle is hardly won. Organic farming is not merely a matter of applying educational techniques, but rather a value system, a world view, which needs to be understood and embraced as a philosophy, a way to be in the world, with the world. As producers refine their techniques, and the public continues to be educated, the market for organic wines in the United States can only continue to grow.

La Suvera, Pievescola, Italy

La Suvera is a residential farm that belongs to the family of the Marquis Ricci Paracciani Bergamini and was once the residence of Pope Julius II. Situated in the town of Pievescola di Casole d'Elsa between Florence and Siena, the area is known for its constant average temperature, which provides optimal conditions for growing wine grapes. Certain peculiarities make la Suvera "some of the best enological expressions of Tuscany."

In 1507, Pope Julius II was presented the La Suvera fortress, and changed it into a Renaissance-style villa. When the pope died, the property was inherited by his family and was eventually passed on to the Marquis Ricci Paracciani Bergamini family

Their certified organic red wine, Rango Rosso, is made from a combination of 70 percent Sangiovese, 16 percent Canaiolo, 8 percent Cabernet Sauvignon, 3 percent Merlot, and 3 percent Cigliegiolo, and is vinified according to the techniques typical of the area of the Siena hills. The wine is matured for a year in oak casks, followed by one year in the bottle. The result is "a typical Tuscan wine, aromatic, pleasant, soft and harmonious which can also be further aged in the bottle for two to three years, and even longer in the case of certain years."

La Suvera also produces a certified organic white wine, "S" Bianco. It is known for its high acidity, which is of benefit in preserving the wine, and is best after it has matured for two years. "S" Bianco is produced from a mixture of 70 percent Trebbiano, 23 percent Malvasia, 4 percent San Colombano, and 3 percent Tokaj and Picolit. The grapes are harvested at the appropriate point of maturation and picked from the bunches before being macerated. The must is then separated from the skin, followed by slow fermentation in stainless steel tanks. After several decantings, the wine rests for about two years before being bottled. "S" Bianco is described as "rich of perfume and flavor, with a full and harmonious body which increases with time."

Robert Haas imports a number of fine wines from France that are made from vineyards organically or biodynamically cultivated. The vineyards are Château de Beaucastel, Coudoulet de Beaucastel, La Coulée de Serrant, Domaine de Torraccia, and Domaine de Trévallon.

Château de Beaucastel produces what many connoisseurs acknowledge as the finest wines of Châteauneuf-du-Pape. The Perrin family was established in 1649, and now the fourth generation of the Perrin family continues a tradition of organic viticulture. No pesticides, chemical fertilizers, or chemical weed killers are used. Only minimal amounts of sulfur–copper are applied to the vineyard.

The Perrins produce a number of premium vintage organically grown wines, one of which is Château de Beaucastel Blanc, made from Roussanne (80 percent), along with a combination of Bourboulenc, Clairette, and Grenache (20 percent). Their red wine, Châteauneuf-du-Pape, is made from a blend of Mourvèdre (more than 30 percent), Counoise, Syrah, Cinsault and as many as nine other varieties (the remaining percentage).

The yields at Beaucastel are extremely low. Each variety is harvested separately to ensure optimum maturity. When the harvest at

Beaucastel reaches the cellar, it is carefully sorted by hand to eliminate any flawed grapes. The grapes are then destemmed and the harvest is flash-heated to help the transfer of aromas and color and to avoid the addition of sulfur dioxide usual in classical vinification. The grapes are then immediately cooled and the vinification is traditional: fermentation on the skins for 15 days, racking of the free-run juice, emptying out the pumice, and pressing.

Each variety is vinified separately to maintain its own character and originality, and when fermentation is finished each wine is carefully tasted before making a single blend. The wine is then relocated to large oak barrels to age for about one and a half years before bottling.

These organic wines are unrefined and unfiltered, and after only two or three years in the bottle, will throw a sediment, making decantation necessary. According to wine expert Robert Parker, Jr., "The results are stunning. The red wine is usually a black–ruby or purple color, loaded with layers of fruit, tannin, and a multitude of fascinating scents and aromas . . . age, usually a minimum of six to ten years, brings forth its majestic richness and compelling array of aromas." He adds, "Their introduction in 1986 of an astonishing wine called Roussanne-Cuvée Vieilles Vignes has established a new benchmark for how complex and brilliant a white wine from the southern Rhône can be. Both the 1986 and 1988 exhibited smoky, hazelnut, and pineapple-scented bouquets, honeyed, luscious fruit, and considerable length. Expect these two wines to close up after one to two years in the bottle, and then blossom in six to ten years."

Coudoulet de Beaucastel is part of the same vineyard as Château de Beaucastel; the only difference is that they are separated by a road that acts as a border between the appellations Châteauneuf-du-Pape and Côtes du Rhône. As anyone who drinks Rhône wines knows, "the Perrins irrefutably produce the longest-lived red wine of the southern Rhône," states Parker. He believes the Coudoulet de Beaucastel, by the standards of Châteauneuf-du-Pape, would be considered among the top ten or twelve wines of the appellation.

La Coulée de Serrant is a domaine covering 17 acres; it lies on the north bank of the Loire River in Anjou, part of the larger, but still obscure, wine-producing region of Savennières. The region is known for producing dry white wines from the Chenin Blanc grape. The vineyards of la Coulée de Serrant have been planted with grapevines continuously for the past six centuries. The vines average around 30 years of age. The entire vineyard has been cultivated with biodynamic methods since 1985. Biodynamics exclude weedkillers, chemical fertilizers, as well as synthetic treating agents, including all insecticides. Also, this special method discourages vines obtained through clonal breeding.

According to the owner, Madame A. Joly, biodynamic viticulture reinforces the vivification of the soil through the use of composts in harmony with specific biodynamic compounds—achillea (sulfur, potash), chamomile (calcium), nettle (iron), oak (lime), valerian (phosphorus)—and through the spraying of minute quantities per hectare (2.4 acres) of such compounds that are energized and sprayed at very precise times; i.e., in sync with cosmic rhythms.

The Moon, during its 29-day rotation around the Earth, travels past the 12 zodiac constellations. These constellations exert four types of influence and promote either leaf growth (water signs: Cancer, Scorpio, Pisces, times that are particularly suitable for leafy vegetables, for example), root growth (earth signs: Capricorn, Virgo, Taurus, these dates being suitable for root vegetables), blooming (light signs: Aquarius, Gemini, Libra), or fruit development (heat signs: Aries, Sagittarius, Leo). Those are the dates chosen for scheduling the work on the vineyard soil. Each of the three signs in the water, earth, light and heat categories presents its own specific characteristics. The Leo sign, for instance, is linked to the reproductive forces. Weeding a vineyard on a bioenergized soil two or three times yearly during that period will double the size of grape seeds, thereby naturally raising the tannic content of the wine. Joly continues to explain that only Bordeaux mixture and nonprocessed powdered sulfur, which are very beneficial to a proper fecundation of the blossoms, are acceptable in biodynamics.

La Coulée de Serrant shows Chenin Blanc at its best: "full-bodied, rich with flavors of peaches and spices, balanced and clean, with the ability to improve in the bottle for years," reports Thomas Matthews in *The Wine Spectator*. Other wine experts agree. "The Coulée de Serrant is perhaps the finest wine of the Loire Valley and one of the greatest in all of

France," states Michel Dovaz, president of the Institut Œnologique de France. Hugh Johnson, in his book, *L'Atlas du Vin,* writes, "[La Coulée de Serrant] illustrates the effect of an exceptional exposure which . . . gives an exceptional wine." *Gault-Millau* describes it as "surely one of the five best dry white wines of France." It is no wonder that La Coulée de Serrant has received its own *Appellation d'Origine Contrôlée.*

Located in a magnificent natural setting, between the mountains and the Tyrrhenian Sea, 10 kilometers to the north of Porto-Vecchio

(which means old port) in the south of Corsica is Domaine de Torraccia. The proprietor, Christian Imbert, spent 15 years in Chad leading the nomadic life of a trader collecting and exporting local products, until 20 years ago, when he planted 80 acres of vines on the granite hillsides. Using only the highest quality plants, his objective from the beginning was to create a vineyard capable of producing a top quality cru.

The variety of grapes planted are for the most part the traditional vines of Corsica. In the rosé, Niellucciu, Sciaccarellu, Grenache, and Cinsault are blended. The vines are trained on iron wires and cultivated in the traditional manner: organically grown without chemical fertilizers, weeding formulas or synthetic pesticides. Each year at the beginning of September, the rows are plowed with lupin, and the following year with vetch and rye, which, during March, become humus. The vines are plowed and worked by hand on the row. The only treatments used are the "bouillie bordelaise" (washing to remove moss, mildew, etc., from vines and casks) and sulfur powder. Production is controlled, at less than 2,000 liters per acre, and the harvest is done only by hand. Only estate grapes are vinified and bottled in the cellar of this domaine.

The rosé can be described as "dry, lively, and fruity with a slight taste of 'pierre-à-fusil' [flint]," and preferably is consumed young. *Wine and Spirits* recommended it and described it as possessing a "wild bouquet of berries . . . good balance with a long perfumed finish. Very well made and very appealing country wine."

Domaine de Trévallon is located in the Coteaux d'Aix-en-Provence, one of the hottest places in France. There is little or no topsoil and the granite and volcanic rocks need to be broken up with dynamite. To avoid burning the vines, owner Aloi Dürrbach plants on north-facing slopes. Yields are small, and the wines are fermented in tanks but are swiftly transferred into oak barrels. There is no filtering or fining.

Although not written on the label, Trévallon wines are organically grown. Every few years a little sheep manure is spread on the soil, and the barest minimum of sulfur is used in bottling. However, Dürrbach has not wished to subscribe to one of the organic labeling institutions because he is afraid that it might lead to a change in his clientele.

Dürrbach has achieved success by flaunting convention. He makes his wine with 60 percent Cabernet Sauvignon and 40 percent Syrah, the idea of which came to him after reading Dr. Guyot's 1868 classic *Étude du Vignoble de France*. Today, Dürrbach is one of only a few men in the Northern Hemisphere to make such a blend. Robert Parker, Jr., states in the *Wine Advocate* that, "The wine, first made in 1977, has improved in quality yearly . . . it is a wine with the magnificent perfume of Penfold's Grange Hermitage or the Hermitage La Chapelle, and the intensity of a Guigal La Mouline. . . . The 1982 is exceptional, the 1983 is superb and has 10–15 years of life ahead of it, the 1984 is one of the best 1984's made in France, and the very fine 1985 is somewhere in style between the explosive 1982 and classic 1983. . . . Move fast on Trévallon—his wines are unquestionably about to become very famous."

Robert Kacher Selections

Robert Kacher represents 40 growers throughout France. Only the finest wines are selected for exporting to the United States. Kacher states that he bases his selections on the quality of the wines, not on the fact that they are grown with conventional or organic methods. Among his selections, he does offer wines from one proprietor in Provence who believes it is important to promote his product as free of synthetic chemicals: Domaine Richeaume. It is located in the appellation Côtes de Provence, a region known for yielding excellent wines.

Domaine Richeaume is a 26-acre vineyard, almost half of which is planted with Cabernet Sauvignon grapes. After vinification, the wines are aged in new 225-liter barrels for 20 months. Absolutely first-class wines are produced at Richeaume. In addition, their vineyard is organically grown without the use of herbicides, insecticides, or other synthetic substances. They produce Syrah, Cuvée (traditional), Cabernet

Sauvignon, and Rosé. Henning Hoesch is proprietor of the Domaine. Twenty years ago, Hoesch left Yale, sold his family business in Europe, and began planting vineyards in the foothills of Mt. Saint Victorie. Today, his wines have been considered by some as the "Léoville Las Cases" of the Côtes de Provence.

Terry Theise Selections

Terry Theise imports and distributes a number of fine wines from Germany. In particular, his organically grown wines include those from Weingut Brüder Dr. Becker and Weingut Günter Wittmann.

Weingut Brüder Dr. Becker produces certified organically grown wines on their estate located in the Rhône Valley in the small village of Ludwigshöhe, located three miles south of Oppenheim in the State of Rhineland Palatinate. The estate developed from a small farming homestead and has been owned and operated by the Pfeffer family since the 18th century.

The Pfeffers dedicate themselves to producing quality wines using organic methods because it avoids damaging the environment. In addition, Lotte Pfeffer believes that wine ought to be respected and not

shoved around. She uses no pumps or centrifuges. "We work with the time factor," she states. "We let time see to clarification and fining. We don't like agitating the wine."

In abiding with the principles of organic farming, crop yield at this vineyard is restricted to 7,000 liters per 2.4 acres through pruning and fertilization. In addition, crops are rotated with ground-covering greens and are conditioned and fertilized with organic nutrients. A small amount of sulfur is applied. The wines are handled very carefully in small barrels during fermentation; they mature primarily in wooden casks and are stored in cellars at ideal temperatures.

Adherence to the above standards is monitored by the German Federal Association of Ecological Vineyards. Weingut Brüder Dr. Becker is an active member of the Association of Organic Wine Growers in Rheinhessen and the estate is under the control of the "Bundökologischer Weinhau." It is also a member of the respected Association of German Prädikatswein Estates.

Association of German Prädikatswein Estates Upgrades Their Standards

Many of Germany's top producers have recently upgraded their standards to improve their wines and the environment. Under the auspicies of the Association of German Prädikatswein Estates (VDP) their 170 members are now required to eliminiate the use of all insecticides and herbicides on their vineyards, as well as to cut back fungicide use to minimal levels. Also in an effort to increase quality, they are required to cut back on yields per acre. These rules took effect for the 1991 vintage. In an interview with Thomas Matthews, New York Bureau Chief of the *Wine Spectator*, Prince Michael zu Salm-Salm, president of the association, stated, "We hope one day to arrive at viticulture with no chemicals at all, except for the traditional use of copper sulfate." The association includes many of Germany's most prestigious wine estates. A special capsule identified with the VDP logo will appear on all wines approved by the association (Matthews, 1991).

Their 1988 Dienheimer Tafelstein Scheurebe *Spätlese* is a prime example of the quality they produce. It is very Riesling-like, with just a hint of Scheu tang. It is also described as possessing a "classy, texturous palate, compact, just lavish in its charm but delicate and lissome [with] a touch of melon and currant."

The vineyard's distinctive wines are made from pure Riesling, Silvaner, and Scheurebe grapes, which are typical for the area; fruity and light, yet full of flavor. Sixty percent of the vintage ranges in the dry to semi-dry categories. The main volume of the vintage is reported to lie in the high-grade segment of *Qualitätswein mit Prädikat*.* Being members of the Verband Okologisches Weinbau (Association of Organic Wine Growers), their newer vintage wines are to be designated with a special seal identifying them as such.

Weingut Günter Wittmann, an estate in Rheinhessen, was discovered by Theise through Scheuermann's classification. Wittmann produces a fine selection of premium organically grown wines and is a member of an association of organic farmers, a few of which are vintners. When asked why he changed over to organic methods, he stated, "I want to give my son a healthy soil for his inheritance. . . . [In addition], we don't make wines ecologically because they're easier to sell, but because we feel it makes better wine."

Wittmann produces eight organically grown wines, all in the high-grade category *Qualitätswein mit Prädikat*: Bechtheimer Hasensprung Huxelrebe *Spätlese*, Westhofener Kirschspiel Scheurebe *Spätlese*, Weisser Riesling *Kabinett* Trocken, Westhofener Mörstein Riesling *Spätlese* Halbtrocken, Westhofener Mörstein Riesling *Spätlese* Trocken, Westhofener Aulerde Riesling Extra Brut Sekt, Westhofener Steingrube Albalonga *Beerenauslese*, and Westhofener Steingrube

---

* Qualitätswein mit Prädikat (quality wine with special attributes). Under this grade of wines, no sugar can be added to the must to increase the alcohol. Must, sugar, and alcohol content have to reach certain levels to obtain the *Prädikat* quality grades. They are *Kabinett, Spätlese, Auslese, Beerenauslese, Eiswein, and Trockenbeerenauslese (TBA)*.

Albalonga *Trockenbeerenauslese*. In the cellar the wines are left with minimal interruption. Any sweetness they contain results from "spontaneously interrupted fermentation," he states. No centrifuges are used, no yeast cultures are applied—all the wines are exactly as nature made them.

Weygandt–Metzler Importing

Weygandt–Metzler imports some exceptional organic wines from France; in particular, those of Jean Pierre Frick. The Frick family has been cultivating vines in Pfaffenheim for at least twelve generations. Growing their grapes on the flanks of the Vosges foothills has yielded distinctive wine, for the region is known for its extreme diversity of soils. Each variety of grape is planted in the soil appropriate to its characteristics.

In 1970 the domaine was converted over to organic methods. The first use of biodynamic agriculture began in 1981. From the 1986 harvest on, the domaine has received the special Demeter certification for its wines. In Greek mythology, Demeter is the goddess of the fruitful soil and of the operations of agriculture.

Frick believes organic wines are better assimilated by the human organism, and that there is a more profound difference between these wines and those cultivated by conventional methods. "Our planet as a whole benefits from viticulture that is more respectful of the environment," he states.

The regular use of biodynamic techniques, which involves working in harmony with cosmic rhythms and forces, stimulates the beneficial effects of the sun, and strengthens plant resistance to disease and parasites. Only organically composted materials are brought to the soil. Hand tilling and weeding, alternating rows of sod and mulching, are the alternatives chosen to chemical herbicides. Powder preparations from infusions of the horsetail or nettle plant, very diluted gruel, and sulfur powder are used on Frick's vines to protect them from rot and mildew.

Optimal maturity and limited yield renders chaptalization (adding sugar to the must) unnecessary for nearly all cuvées. After the drawing off, the musts are fermented in their own yeasts. The development of the wine is only punctuated by one or two rackings and by a minute addition of sulfur, to the exclusion of all other additives or stabilizers. A minimal natural cellulose filtration just before bottling concludes the six to nine months spent in huge oak casks for the secondary fermentation. Although there is a minimum of intervention in the wines' natural development, it is constant vigilance that preserves the essential life of the wine.

Situated on a geological fault, a mosaic of soils in which limestone predominates offers ideal conditions for the full blossoming of each of the Alsatian grape varieties. Varieties that this winery produces include several Pinot Blancs, Gewürztraminers, and Pinot Gris, and a Muscat, Sylvaner, and Riesling.

The wines can be characterized as dry, pure, and complex in bouquet and flavor, and are not drowned out by residual sugar and added alcohol. No pesticides, fungicides, or herbicides are used; the grape-growing and winemaking are strictly natural.

These wines are available in Maryland, New Jersey, New York, and Washington, D.C., and possibly in the near future, Arizona and California.

Conclusion: A Toast To a Healthier Society and Environment

One may surmise from the information submitted by the organic wine representatives that the majority switched to organic methods because they work toward a healthier society and environment. Some producers are using organic methods because they believe it increases the quality of the wine, or because of an increase in market demand for the product. Whatever their motivation, one thing is certain: never before has it been so necessary to nurture the Earth and the life upon it. Our actions must be supportive of life, otherwise physical and spiritual laws are leading us to conclude that a purging is inevitable, as history and ancient history remind us. Principles such as those proposed by Isaac Newton also lend credence to our fate: "For every action, there is an equal and opposite reaction."

If the action is buying organic wine and other organic products, then the end result is more agricultural land that is converted to organic methods, therefore supporting more life and creating more stable ecosystems. An equal and opposite reaction is that we in turn will be supported in our life. For example, organic farming is drought resistant, prevents topsoil erosion, yields equal or greater amounts of food, yields food with a greater nutritional value, attracts and sustains a wide variety of beneficial insects and natural predators, and eliminates the need for detrimental agricultural chemicals. The benefits do not stop with the Earth. "When a consumer buys organic, a domino falls and affects a chain of reactions. Consumer choice supports a network of farmers, brokers, processors, distributors, retailers, and restauranteurs committed to conducting business in a globally responsible manner" (*OGWA Newsletter,* 1991). For those who consume this healthier food the end result translates into stronger immune systems, less sickness, fatigue and stress while bringing about more productiveness. The ultimate result is a richer, fuller, and happier life.

Collectively, we humans have yet to perform the greatest experiment—working with the environment and nurturing it. In a society where this took place, it is very possible that we would reach our ultimate potential as human beings in terms of developing our bodies and minds. The world as we know it would be unlike anything ever experienced: a "heaven" filled with life. Peace and love would result from the stability that it brings.

New understandings about how humankind interacts with and affects the physical world are finally beginning to emerge in today's scientific arena. In contrast, dogmatic theories that fail to fully explain the universal mechanisms that affect every individual's life are crumbling, and so are the foundations of civilization. We are witnessing a growing world economic crisis and at the same time an increase in the intensity, as well as number, of "natural" catastrophes. In these areas that are plagued with destruction, wilderness is on the verge of being reestablished as it has done throughout the ages. This is the lesson that we have yet to fully understand. This is the knowledge that could very well lead humankind to its truest ascent. An understanding of our relationship with the physical world is the foundation in which the concept of organic production is inspired.

Organic wine that enhances one's health, therefore, is "a living, fermented health food beverage." For a truly living microecology to exist within the wine, it must be produced from grapes that are free of synthetic pesticides and produced without the use of chemical additives—both of which have been known to destroy the very life within the wine that makes it so beneficial for one's health. The wine must also be produced with the highest quality standards. This book has demonstrated that the majority of organic wine growers and producers fulfill these standards. The conclusion can only be that the greatest positive and the least negative effects from wine consumption are the result of consuming the most natural, uncontaminated product.

Proper use—one to two glasses per day at most, and drunken slowly, preferably before or during a meal—also enhances the beneficial effects from wine's consumption. One may even go as far as to say that consuming it with a spiritual mind-frame—a loving, moral, ethical, and knowledgable mind-set—will greatly add to its beneficial effects.

The next time you go shopping, if you do not already buy organic wine or other organic products, try them out and see how much better you feel. In addition, your dollar will be going toward making the world a better place for all.

Wine Tasting Notes

The following descriptions are a composite of notes taken by a group of five people during nine months of wine tastings. Many of the wines, particularly those with no added sulfites, were sampled several times to test for consistency. However, they are only meant to be educated opinions of individuals with well-developed palates.

These notes review approximately 85 percent of all organic wines, both domestic and imported, that were available for purchase in the United States before this book's publication. The producers' names are alphabetized under each of the categories and are italicized for easy identification.

The price ranges used in the notes are based on the suggested retail prices. Please keep in mind that actual prices may vary, based on the wholesaler's and retailer's markup and the state in which the wine is sold. Wines that are sold in a state other than where they were produced or imported to generally are higher because of shipping and transportation charges, and therefore may fall in a higher price range. For example, if you buy a wine in California that is produced in that state, the wine will probably be less expensive than in Arizona (by as much as $2 per bottle), and therefore may fall in a lower price range. In the notes that follow, the prices used to determine the range for each of the wines include the extra markup. The ranges are as follows: under $7 is inexpensive, $7 to $8 is fairly inexpensive, $9 to $12 is reasonable, $13 to $16 is moderate, $17 to $25 is high priced, and more than $25 is expensive. For information on growing and processing methods for a particular winery, consult the index.

Domestic Reds

Cabernet Sauvignon

Bellerose's Cuvée Cabernet Sauvignon, vintage 1985, is a crystalline, very appealing, deep, dark purple-red at 12.9 percent alcohol. Its enticing, complex bouquet has a positive fruity fragrance. Dry, stimulating, tart, and medium-bodied, this Cabernet blend is well balanced and moderately priced.

Briceland's Cabernet Sauvignon, vintage 1988, is an unclouded, deep garnet with 12.8 percent alcohol. An enchanting, complex, powerful bouquet with a hint of vanilla and berry makes it almost like a Zinfandel. Very dry with very soft tannins and hints of oak, butter, and vanilla complement the full-bodied, very well balanced, smooth savor. The good overall quality will improve with time; this is a moderately priced Cabernet.

Coturri's Cabernet Sauvignon, vintage 1988, shows careful handling with its alcohol content of 14.7 percent. By sight it is a crystalline, deep, dark ruby with an alluring, positive and identifiable aromatic fragrance. Very dry but invigorating and full bodied with very good balance, this superior wine has no added sulfites and is moderately priced.

Fitzpatrick's Cab[2], nonvintage, is a deep garnet and has 13 percent alcohol. A mixture of 50 percent Ruby Cabernet and 50 percent Cabernet Sauvignon, the smooth bouquet with a slight bite accompanies a very dry plum flavor that is mildly astringent but pleasant. Reasonably priced, this wine can be drunk now and should improve with aging.

Fitzpatrick's Estate-Bottled Cabernet Sauvignon, vintage 1987, contains 13.5 percent alcohol. A deep purple with a pleasant, wildberry bouquet is matched with a wildberry, spicy, and buttery savor. The very good balance will improve with age, making this reasonably priced wine a very good buy.

Frey's 1988 Cabernet Sauvignon radiates a dark ruby with 13.7 percent alcohol. The pleasant aroma has a touch of wood and pepper. Dry and spicy, the refreshing full-bodied flavor is distinctively Cabernet. Its good balance and moderate price make it especially attractive to those who desire a wine with no added sulfites.

The Hess Collection's Cabernet Sauvignon, vintage 1987, is a translucent deep ruby with an alcohol content of 12.5 percent. It has an attractive, pleasant bouquet with a woody scent. A dry, refreshing medium body hints of barrel and stems that should improve with aging. The good balance should also improve with time for this high-priced wine. Tannins with a flat acidity contrast the very sweet, dessert wine flavor, which is inadvisable for those with blood sugar problems.

La Rocca's Cabernet Sauvignon, vintage 1987, is also portlike in its sweetness and has an alcohol content of 14.5 to 15 percent. Opaque, dark purple-red, it delivers an appealing aroma and is moderately priced.

Las Montañas's Cabernet Sauvignons, vintages 1985 and 1986, are deep, dark red with 13 percent alcohol. Their medium body possesses a full-spectrum, mildly fruity fragrance. Dry with low tannins, they are smooth and rich-flavored with a fruity berry zest. The good balance is enhanced by no added sulfites. Moderately priced, they are fine Cabernets that will improve with age.

Olson's Cabernet Sauvignon, vintage 1986, is an opaque, deep ruby with an alcohol content of 13.2 percent. Its delightful bouquet gratifies, with a hint of cedarwood that should improve with aging. Very dry with marked acidity and a full body, it is an attractive wine that is reasonably priced.

Merlot

Bellerose's Merlot, vintage 1986, contains 12.7 percent alcohol and is a translucent, deep purple. Its appealing, complex aroma is positive and easily identifiable as a Merlot. The good balance and moderate price of this organic–commercial blend make it attractive.

La Rocca's Merlot, vintage 1986, has 17 percent alcohol. Sweet and portlike, this Merlot is a deep, dark purple-red. The smell is powerful and positive, but has a hint of yeast. The light body tastes very sweet, but is somewhat offset by a dry tannic background. Moderately priced, it may be considered a dessert wine, which makes it inadvisable for people with blood sugar problems.

Olson's Merlot, vintage 1989, is one of their best wines, with 13.5 percent alcohol. Its translucent garnet and positive, pleasantly complex bouquet allure. The tannins are dry, making a dry to medium-dry wine with a flat acidity. The extended taste of its medium to full body is very well balanced and will improve with age. A reasonable price makes Olson's fine Merlot even more attractive.

Pinot Noir

Briceland's Pinot Noir, vintage 1989, radiates an opaque red. The mild berry bouquet accompanies its dry, full-flavored, medium body with a hint of pepper. The good balance will improve with aging, and it is moderately priced.

Cameron's Pinot Noir, vintage 1990, has 12.5 percent alcohol. Radiating a transulucent ruby, the light-bodied, semi-dry, very fruity taste is matched with a plumlike bouquet. Being a new vintage, aging will improve this no-additive, no-sulfite, reasonably priced wine.

Coturri's Pinot Noir, Horn Vineyards, vintage 1989, with an alcohol content of 14.6 percent reflects careful handling. By sight a brilliant deep, dark purple, this Pinot Noir has an outstanding, gratifying and identifiable polished berry fragrance. Dry with soft tannins and medium to full bodied, its close-to-perfect balance should improve with aging. A work of art at a moderate price and no added sulfites, it is sure to be attractive to the most discriminating palate, as well as to people who are sulfite-sensitive.

Frey's Pinot Noir, vintage 1990, is a transparent red and has an alcohol content of 13.6 percent. A sharp, mildly fruity fragrance is accompanied by a dry, medium-bodied, somewhat refreshing acidity that make a good wine. Moderately priced and fairly well balanced, this wine will improve with aging.

Nevada County Wine Guild's Pinot Noir, vintage 1989, contains 12.4 percent alcohol. A lucid medium-deep purple red with an alluring and delightfully complex fragrance is companion to a positive fruitiness. Dry with dry tannins, an exhilarating balance enhances its medium body. Priced in the fairly inexpensive range, this wine is a good value and contains no added sulfites.

Octopus Mountain's Pinot Noir, vintage 1989, has 12.5 percent alcohol. A raisiny bouquet is comrade to a raisiny, smooth savor. A very good balance and moderate price produce a good value with a potential for improvement with aging.

Ponderosa's Pinot Noir, vintage 1989, has an alcohol content of 13.5 percent. A deep, opaque purple-red with an attractive aroma offers evidence of oak aging. It is dry, refreshing, and medium bodied with a hint of berry. A fairly good balance, offset by a slight taste of stems and oak, suggests that it will improve with age. Moderately priced and no added or detectable sulfites make a wine especially attractive to sulfite-sensitive persons and those who want wines without additives.

Zinfandel

Coturri's Zinfandel, vintage 1989, with an alcohol content of 14.7 percent, reflects careful handling. The brilliant deep, dark purple is matched by an outstanding, gratifying, and identifiable polished berry essence. Dry with soft tannins and medium to full bodied, its balanced taste makes it close to perfect, and it should improve with aging. Reflecting the work of an artist and moderately priced with no added sulfites, it is a Zinfandel worth every cent.

Frey's 1989 Zinfandel is a deep, opaque ruby with 13.3 percent alcohol. A mild berry scent is matched by a medium-bodied, dry, distinctive berry flavor of zinfandels. Reasonably priced, a good balance and no added sulfites make an attractive wine, especially for those who desire no added sulfites.

La Rocca's Botrytes Zinfandel, vintage 1987, has an alcohol content of 13.8 percent. Translucent, medium-deep purple-red in color, its bouquet is alluring, positive, and complex. A medium-dry taste with soft tannins and expensive price make it the best of the La Rocca line.

Las Montañas's Zinfandels, 1983, 1985, 1986, and 1988 vintages, are a deep ruby with 13 percent alcohol. A very attractive, distinctively zinfandel berry bouquet is matched with a medium-dry, intensely flavorful wild fruity berry flavor. Rich, soft, full-bodied character makes a fine wine that is well balanced with no added sulfites. Aging potential and a moderate price make a very alluring wine that will be in demand.

Olson's Zinfandel, vintage 1988, has an alcohol content of 12.6 percent. An unclouded deep dark purple is accompanied by a complex alluring aroma with a hint of cedarwood. The tannins are dry and soft, and the acidity is full spectrum and brawny. A medium body complements the extended well-balanced, somewhat buttery savor; this wine should improve with aging. Reasonably priced, Olson's Zinfandel is a good value.

Orleans Hill's 1990 Zinfandel Nouveau radiates a deep, dark purple with 12 percent alcohol. The intense blackberry aroma of this full-bodied wine is accompanied by a tart, dry, berry–plum taste. Though made to drink immediately, its very tannic nature may improve with aging. The good balance and fairly inexpensive price make it worth a try.

San Pietro Vara's Zinfandel, vintage 1984, sheds a seductive garnet that suggests a healthy grape and has an alcohol content of 13.5 percent. Dry, light bodied with a mild berry flavor that is better left to breathe, it has a satisfying scent. The tannins are fairly strong, but are the result of the method used, which includes not adding sulfites. Moderately priced, this wine has fairly good balance and should improve with age.

Topolos's 1988 Zinfandels represent some of their best wines. The alcohol content of the Ultimo and the Rossi Ranch varieties are 13 percent, and the Sonoma variety, 12.9 percent. Each is a deep purple-red with an enjoyable, slightly fruity aroma and will improve with aging. Ultimo is smooth for a fairly young wine and is the best red of the Topolos line. The Sonoma variety tastes of cedar and needs more aging than the other varieties. Rossi Ranch and Sonoma Zinfandels are good values but need more aging than Ultimo, which is also a reasonably priced wine.

Other Reds

Coturri's Albarello, vintage 1989, balances at 12 percent alcohol. Coming from the bottom of the barrel of the other Coturri wines, it is strong in hard tannins and needs at least five or more years of aging. The wait may be worth the fairly inexpensive price.

Frey's Carignane, vintage 1989, is an opaque deep ruby and contains 13.3 percent alcohol. A milder bouquet than their other carignane (Organic Red), it has a softer finish to match. The very dry, round, and very refreshing ambience brings about a well-balanced, good value, reasonably priced wine that should age well.

Frey's Organic Red, vintage 1989, contains 11.6 percent alcohol and sheds a cloudy deep ruby. The sweet aroma of this 100 percent Carignane is fruity and fairly mild, contrasting the very dry, yet fruity, mildly sweet and tart tang. Mild tannins that should improve with age make a refreshing medium-bodied, well-balanced wine of good value at a reasonable price.

Frey's Syrah, vintage 1989, reflects an opaque, deep red with an alcohol content of 11.7 percent. The mildly fruity scent and medium body with a dry, acidic refreshing bite make a moderately fine wine. A fairly good balance goes hand in hand with its reasonable price.

Hallcrest's El Dorado Barbera, vintage 1990, contains 12.5 percent alcohol. The deep purple hue is accompanied by a pleasant acidic aroma. A mild berry, fruity, slightly acidic flavor offsets the astringent tannins. Aging of this new wine will make its reasonable price a good value.

Ponderosa's Red Table Wine, vintage 1990, has an alcohol content of 12.5 percent. Ruby in color, this red has almost no scent, but its dry, mild berry, fruity flavor makes it desirable. A potential for improvement with age and a moderate price are attractive.

Prager's Royal Escort Port, vintage 1988, contains a hefty 19.2 percent alcohol (fortified*). The deep, dark garnet accompanies the full-bodied, semi-sweet essence with nuances of plum, raspberry, and cherry. The exceptional handling of 100 percent Petite Sirah, which is unfined, unfiltered, and has no added sulfites, fashions a stimulating superior apertif port that is worth the very expensive price.

Prager's Noble Companion Port, with 18.8 percent alcohol (fortified), radiates a deep, dark garnet. As a semi-dry port, made from 100 percent Cabernet Sauvignon, the low residual sugar and good balance are a pleasant surprise. The plum scent is matched with the taste of plums, prunes, and raisins. Though not as good as Prager's other Port, it is still handled very well and should improve with age, being a later release.

San Pietro Vara's Charbono, vintage 1985, contains 12 percent alcohol and is fairly strong, pungent, and tart. Though it is not as good as their 1983 vintage, which received a gold medal, the fairly good balance and moderate price make it worth a try.

San Pietro Vara's Gamay, vintage 1986, has an alcohol content of 11.5 percent and is mildly sweet and fruity. A smooth flavor with some dry tannins should improve by aging another year or two. Not totally organic (some commercial grapes were added), the good balance and fairly inexpensive price are a plus.

Topolos's Alicante-Bouschet has 13 percent alcohol for its 1987, 1988, and 1989 vintages. These unclouded, deep purple-red wines release a positive, pleasant fruity fragrance. The dry, medium body is offset with high tannin levels that contribute a woody, tart taste. As with the other

---

* Fortified wine signifies that additional alcohol—usually in the form of grape brandy—was added after fermentation.

Topolos wines, aging will improve the quality of this reasonably priced varietal.

Topolos's Grand Noir, a Rhône-style red, vintage 1988, contains 13 percent alcohol. This deep, dark purple-red releases a mild, agreeable fruity bouquet. The bone-dry, tart flavor, however, is marred by astringent tannins that smell of barrel and stems. As a result, aging for at least another five years is advisable for this reasonably priced wine.

Topolos's Petite Sirah, vintage 1988, has 13 percent alcohol. A deep purple-red is complemented by an attractive, slightly fruity scent. The dry, medium-bodied taste is offset by excessive tannins. Moderately priced, aging for at least five years should improve its character.

Domestic Rosés and Blushes

Badger Mountain's Blush, vintage 1990, contains 10.3 percent alcohol. The pale reddish-pink wine brings forth a medium sweet and mildly fruity taste with a soft scent of vanilla. As one of the better blushes, it is even more attractive with the inexpensive price.

Fitzpatrick's Sierra Dreams is a transparent, medium red with an appealing, agreeable fruity fragrance at 11.5 percent alcohol. The 1990 vintage has one of the most beautiful labels in the business. The medium-dry taste, and the light to medium body with mild, candy apple flavor contribute to its good balance and attractiveness. This Blanc de Noir is a good value because it is fairly inexpensive. First-time wine drinkers will be pleased.

Frey's Blush, vintage 1990, a pale, transparent red, has 12.6 percent alcohol. The very mild aroma possesses hints of fruit, matched by a mild, somewhat refreshing flavor. It has a moderately good balance and is fairly inexpensive.

Octopus Mountain's Wild Rose, 1988 vintage, has an alcohol content of 11.9 percent and radiates a clear pale red. The inviting, positive fragrance enhances the light- to medium-bodied flavor. With good balance, this wine is a fine domestic rosé and priced inexpensively.

Paul Thomas's Crimson Rhubarb is a transparent, pale pink with 12 percent alcohol. A pleasant and slightly fruity smell is matched with a medium-dry, tart, light body. Though not actually a rosé, the color suggests that it is. Overall it might be said that rhubarb, which requires added sugar, is not an ingredient one would use to produce a premium wine. Fairly inexpensive, Crimson Rhubarb may sell to some, in particular those who wish no added or detected sulfites.

Ponderosa's Vin Rosé, vintage 1989, contains 12 percent alcohol. It is a clear, pale red with a slight, pleasant fruity aroma. No added or detected sulfites make an attractive rosé to sulfite-sensitive individuals and those who want wines without additives. Medium dry, light and refreshing, this wine has a good balance and is a good value at an inexpensive price.

Domestic Whites

Chardonnay

Badger Mountain's Chardonnays, vintages 1989 and 1990, are a transparent golden yellow with 11.7 percent and 10.7 percent alcohol, respectively. Medium-dry with a mildly fruity fragrance, their medium-bodied flavor is slightly fruity and mildly refreshing, with a hint of yeast in the 1989. The 1990 has an improved balance, bouquet, and flavor. The reasonable price makes the 1990 alluring.

Blue Heron Lake's Chardonnay is from Wild Horse Valley, a name that hints at its superior quality. With an alcohol content of 12.5 percent, the 1988 vintage has a strong golden color and a fruity, very gratifying fragrance. Exceptionally rich and strong bodied with a hearty, lasting finish combined with oak, fruit, vanilla, and butter flavors, this Chardonnay is probably America's best white wine. Moderately priced, it is worth every penny.

Briceland's Chardonnay, vintage 1990, contains 12.8 percent alcohol. A translucent golden yellow, the very mild, medium-dry flavor is fruity with a lingering hint of nitrogen. Priced moderately, this Chardonnay should improve with aging.

The Hess Collection's Chardonnay, vintage 1989, radiates a pale golden yellow with 13 percent alcohol. Its medium body has a bouquet that hints of apples, and a heart that suggests butter, apples, and oak. The good balance, especially with its spectrum of mild sweetness, and the moderate price produce a fine wine that should improve with time.

Hidden Cellar's Chardonnays, vintages 1989 and 1990, contain 13.5 percent alcohol. A transparent golden yellow hue accompanies a sweet, fruity fragrance. Characteristic of a Chardonnay, it is also medium dry and medium to full bodied with a hint of oak. The good balance with aging potential and moderate price make this wine especially attractive.

Nevada County Wine Guild's Chardonnay, vintage 1989, is one of the best American organic Chardonnays and has 12.6 percent alcohol. A crystalline, medium yellow tantalizes with its positive and gratifying bouquet. The medium-dry and enticing savor is accented with a buttery apple background. A fine wine that is fairly inexpensively priced should sell very well.

Octopus Mountain's Chardonnay, vintage 1989, sheds a pale golden yellow with a green tinge, at 13 percent alcohol. A very light and mildly sweet, fruity fragrance matches its mild sweetness, with a short, dry finish. There is a lingering tartness in a medium body that tastes of creamy butter with a hint of rye. This is the best of the Octopus line, and the reasonable price makes it particularly attractive.

Olson's Chardonnay, vintage 1989, is a transparent medium yellow-gold with an alcohol content of 12.8 percent. A slight fruity, clean, and very mild fragrance matches the dry to medium-dry, slight tartness and good balance. This Chardonnay sells at a reasonable price.

Olson's Konrad Estate Chardonnay, vintage 1989, radiates a medium pale yellow hue that is slightly heavy with 12.5 percent alcohol. The enticing, complex, and slightly fruity bouquet is matched with a dry, stimulating, full-bodied ambience. As a very well-balanced, fine wine that is moderately priced, it should please many.

Topolos's Sonoma, Russian River Chardonnay, vintage 1989, is a transparent, pale yellow with 12% alcohol. The fragrance is crisp and delightfully fruity. Its medium-dry, refreshing taste and well-balanced, medium body make this wine attractive at a reasonable price.

Riesling

Badger Mountain's Rieslings, vintages 1989 and 1990, are a transparent golden yellow with alcohol contents of 13.8 percent and 10.3 percent respectively. A light bouquet is paired with a medium-dry, low-acid taste and a medium body. For the 1990 varieties, the Johannisburg is not as dry and clean as the Dry Riesling. Both are an improvement from the previous year's Riesling and are fairly inexpensive.

Briceland's Estate White Riesling, vintage 1989, has 11.8 percent alcohol. A transparent green tinge matches its mildly sweet, fruity, and stimulating round flavor. This is a good summer wine that is moderately priced.

Hallcrest's White Riesling from the Santa Cruz Mountains, vintage 1990, contains 12.7 percent alcohol. The transparent golden yellow is attended by a very mild fragrance and a medium-sweet, fruity full body. A reasonable price with aging potential make it a possible future choice wine.

Olson's Late Harvest Johannisberg Riesling, vintage 1989, can be considered a dessert wine, the alcohol content of which is low (10.5 percent) for a late harvest. A translucent, pale yellow color is accompanied by a clean, pleasing honeyed-lemon smell. The flat acidity with the taste of caramel highlights its fairly good balance. Very sweet, this wine is not recommended for those with blood sugar problems. It is reasonably priced.

Sauvignon Blanc and Fumé Blanc

Bellerose's Sauvignon Blanc, vintage 1987, contains 12.9 percent alcohol and sheds a clear, pale green color. This watery Blanc has a slight fruity scent that is offset by a hint of nitrogen. A medium-dry and light-bodied flavor is countered by a yeasty aftertaste. At a reasonable price, an organic–commercial blend might compete with some commercial brands.

Briceland's Humboldt Sauvignon Blanc, vintage 1990, radiates a transparent gold. With an alcohol content of 13.6 percent, the very mild bouquet is characteristic of the variety and matched by a very dry characteristic flavor. The good balance and moderate price make it attractive.

Fitzpatrick's Eire Ban, vintages 1988 and 1990, are transparent golden yellow with a wide viscosity and 12.5 percent alcohol. An attractive, pleasant aroma with a positive fruity scent go hand in hand with their medium-dry, medium-bodied, crisp clean flavor. The 1990 is a considerable improvement with an appealing acidity that cleanses the palate, making a stimulating and superior, reasonably priced Sauvignon Blanc.

Frey's Sauvignon Blanc, vintage 1990, comes in two varieties, one of which is a late harvest. The alcohol content of the late harvest is 15.2 percent and the other is 13.8 percent. Both have a brilliant pale, golden yellow color. This late-harvest, estate-bottled Blanc has a sweet fruity scent matched by a medium-bodied, sweet, fruity flavor that makes it a dessert wine and not good for those with blood sugar problems. The regular harvest is fruity and medium bodied with a mildly fruity aroma. Both are fairly well balanced, have no added sulfites, and are reasonably priced.

Hallcrest's Sauvignon Blanc, vintage 1990, contains 12 percent alcohol. The characteristic Sauvignon Blanc bouquet is offset by a hint of nitrogen. A pale golden color accompanies a semi-dry, round flavor. Aging may improve this reasonably priced wine.

Olson's Sauvignon Blanc Reserve, vintage 1989, radiates a transparent pale yellow with an alcohol level of 12.5 percent. The clean bouquet and slightly fruity scent satisfy the senses. The taste is medium-dry, refreshing, and light to medium bodied with a good balance. A reasonable price makes it even more appealing.

Olson's 1988 Sauvignon Blanc contains 12.5 percent alcohol and is slightly more pale and has a better taste than the 1989 vintage, suggesting that aging will improve them. Both are reasonably priced.

Organic Wine Works' Fumé Blanc, vintage 1990, has 12 percent alcohol. A pale golden yellow with a pear-accented, full-spectrum aroma accompanies a semi-dry, light body that is slightly tart and acidic but refreshing and pleasant. Fairly inexpensive, no added sulfites and a good balance create a very good value wine that should improve with time.

Topolos's Sauvignon Blanc, vintage 1990, has 12 percent alcohol. It is a transparent pale yellow with a slight sparkle. The alluring fruity scent accents the dry, stimulating, light-bodied, well-balanced taste that hints of oak and butter. It may be considered the best white wine of the Topolos line and is a good value at a reasonable price.

Other Whites

Badger Mountain's Chenin Blanc, vintage 1989, is a pale yellow with 13.9 percent alcohol. A low-acid, mildly fruity aroma is matched with a light-bodied, dry clean taste. This is one of the better Badger wines, and it is fairly inexpensive.

Badger Mountain's Gewürztraminer, vintage 1989, is a pale gold with 12.7 percent alcohol. The sweet, mildly fruity smell is accompanied by a medium-sweet distinctively Gewürtztraminer flavor. This wine is fairly low in sulfites and fairly inexpensive.

Badger Mountain's Sevés, vintages 1989 and 1990, are a transparent yellow and have 12.5 percent and 11.6 percent alcohol, respectively. A very light, peachy bouquet is attended with a dry, low-acid, very light-bodied flavor. The 1990 vintage has improved considerably and also has a more attractive label. They have the lowest sulfites of the line and are fairly inexpensive, making the 1990 very appealing.

Frey's French Colombard, vintage 1990, is a pale golden yellow at 12.6 percent alcohol. A slight fruity aroma matches its light- to medium-bodied, medium-dry refreshing taste. It has a moderately good balance and is fairly inexpensive.

Frey's Gewürztraminers, vintages 1989 and 1990, are a greenish, pale yellow with 11.5 percent and 13.5 percent alcohol, respectively. The 1990 has a mildly sweet aroma with a hint of flowers and a mild earthy taste. The 1989 has a mild, flowery, sweet aroma accompanied by a semi-sweet fruity effervescent flavor. The 1990 was handled more carefully and has a potential for aging another two or three years. Both have a moderately good balance and are reasonably priced.

La Rocca's White Zinfandel, vintage 1986, has an alcohol content of 16.4 percent (fortified). The clouded, tawny color hints at its portlike scent. However, it tastes more like a very sweet sherry or dessert wine, which is inadvisable for those with blood sugar problems. This wine is priced for those with expensive tastes.

Octopus Mountain's Vin Blanc, vintage 1989, contains a 12 percent alcohol content. The transparent, pale and straw-colored hue conveys an enticing, slightly fruity aroma. Medium dry, invigorating, crisp, and tart with a slight sparkle, it is very alluring and leaves a pleasant aftertaste. Good balance and a moderate price also contribute to its attractiveness.

Organic Wine Works' à Notre Mer (to our sea) has no vintage and contains 12 percent alcohol. A transparent pale yellow color accompanies its extremely mild, sweet scent. The tart, acidic flavor is offset by a hint of nitrogen. This medium-dry wine with a fairly good balance and no added sulfites is enhanced by a fairly inexpensive price.

Organic Wine Works' Sémillon, vintage 1990, has 12 percent alcohol and sheds a light golden yellow color. The mildly sweet bouquet and slight flowery scent complement the medium-dry and medium-bodied, distinctly Sémillon flavor, but it is less sweet than most other varieties. A good balance, no added sulfites, and a fairly inexpensive price make this wine a good value that will likely improve with some aging.

Ponderosa's Semi-Sweet Apertif–Satisfaction Plus, vintage 1989, has an alcohol content of 18 percent (fortified). A pale, hazy yellow color conveys an agreeable fruity scent that is offset by a somewhat medicinal smell that is obviously the result of the high alcohol content. This medium-dry to medium-sweet wine has a slight butterscotch and smoky tang—refreshing for such high alcohol levels. The balance is fairly good, and it is reasonably priced. No added sulfites and no detectable sulfur dioxide make it especially attractive to the sulfite-sensitive consumer and those who want wines without additives.

Domestic Sparkling Wine

Briceland's Humboldt Brut Sparkling, vintage 1987, balances at 12.5 percent alcohol. Its fruity bouquet has a mild, yeasty touch. The peachy gold hue is matched by a dry, crisp, flavorful, peachy complex savor that stimulates the appetite. The balanced acidity and good finish make another glass very appealing. Very well balanced and high priced (but very reasonable for a sparkling wine), it is one of America's best sparkling wines and worthy of that day of celebration.

French Reds

André Chaumont's Pere et Fils Mercurey, vintage 1985, contains 12 percent alcohol and is an unclouded, medium purple-red. It delivers an appealing, gratifying fruity fragrance, which accompanies a dry, invigorating, medium-bodied flavor countered by the taste of stems. Its good balance makes a fairly expensive wine that should improve with time.

Château Bousquette, Saint-Chinian Rouge, vintage 1988, radiates an opaque, deep ruby. At 12.5 percent alcohol, its alluring, complex, fruity bouquet matches the dry, peppery, medium body with a marked acidity. The good balance and reasonable price identify it as a good value.

Château de Beaucastel, vintage 1988, has an alcohol level of 13 percent. A transparent, deep ruby-brown accompanies an appealing aroma that offsets a scent of smoke and wood. The invigorating and medium-bodied taste hints of berry and wood. The good balance should improve with time for this expensively priced wine.

Château du Moulin de Peyronin, vintage 1988, comes from the Bordeaux region. Its transparent medium red goes hand in hand with the slightly watery consistency. With a 12 percent alcohol content, it has a clean, pleasant bouquet that is distinctly French, and sells at a reasonable price.

Château la Maubastit, vintage 1988, contains 12 percent alcohol. The wine is garnet, the bouquet smells of smoke, flint, and oak. The mildly sharp, oaky, and tart taste offsets a touch of nitrogen to the flavor. One wonders why the label reads "guaranteed Bordeaux quality," because most wines from that region are better. Aging will improve this reasonably priced wine.

Château Meric, Graves Rouge, Grand Vin de Bordeaux, vintage 1986, has 12 percent alcohol and sheds an opaque medium purple-red. The engaging, satisfying, fruity aroma is matched with a dry, medium-bodied tang that has a short aftertaste and marked acidity. The flavor, offset by a barrel taste, could be improved with age. Otherwise the good balance shows potential with a moderate price tag.

Christian Ducroux's Régnié, Grand Vin du Beaujolais, vintage 1989, contains 12 percent alcohol. It is ruby colored with a pleasing, complex fruity bouquet. The dry, invigorating medium-bodied flavor hints of berries or currants and a robust pepper essence. This well-balanced red could become a fine wine with time and is reasonably priced.

Coudoulet de Beaucastel, vintage 1988, has an alcohol content of 12.5 percent. The transparent, reddish-brown color is matched by a woody aroma. A mild berry flavor counters a tannic and smoky background. Though high priced, the good balance should improve with aging up to ten years or more.

Domaine du Daumas Gassac, vintage 1989, is an opaque ruby with 13 percent alcohol. Its smoky flavor matches the smooth tannins and peppery finish. Medium bodied, this high-priced wine should improve with age.

Domaine de la Gautière en Province, Vin de Pays, no vintage, is a translucent pale ruby with a watery consistency and 12.5 percent alcohol. The aroma conveys a pleasing fruitiness, and the wine's dry, refreshing and light- to medium-bodied flavor hints of pepper. The good balance and fairly inexpensive price make it an adequate wine that should improve with aging.

Domaine de la Jasse, Côtes du Rhône, vintage 1989, contains 13 percent alcohol. A dull medium-red to red-brown color accompanies a very mild pleasant scent with a hint of freshly cut wood. Dry, tart, rich, and medium-bodied with a touch of smoke flavor, this reasonably priced wine should be enhanced by aging.

Domaine de Tavernel's La Sarabande, no vintage, has 12 percent alcohol. The bouquet smells of sweet oak and the color is a deep garnet. It is dry with an oaky and smoky flavor. Aging will improve this wine but without a vintage one can only guess how improved an inexpensively priced wine has become.

Domaine de Trévallon, Coteaux d'Aix en Provence, vintage 1988, contains 12 percent alcohol and is a transparent, deep brick red. An appealing, pleasant aroma hints of berry and wood. Dry and medium bodied with astringent tannins, the flavor possesses a slight flinty aftertaste. The good balance should improve with time and offset the high price.

Domaine des Cedres, Côtes du Rhône, vintage 1987, is a transparent, pale to medium red with 12 percent alcohol. Its nippy, attractive, slightly fruity bouquet accompanies a dry, smoky, light to medium body with hard, dry tannins. The fairly good balance and marked acidity make it a fairly good table wine at a reasonable price.

Domaine du Bas Deffens, Coteaux Varois, vintage 1986, possesses an alcohol content ranging from 11 to 14 percent. It is a clear, dark red and has an attractive fruity aroma offset by a woody sharp scent. This dry, refreshing medium-bodied wine possesses a hint of berry flavor. The fair balance indicates a mediocre wine with aging potential at a reasonable price.

Domaine Richeaume's Cabernet Sauvignons, vintages 1986, 1987, and 1988, have 12.5 percent alcohol. All are a dark garnet with a very dry, smoky, and mildly biting oakiness. The 1988 has more tannins and tartness and needs more aging than the 1987. The 1987 is more developed than 1988 with milder tannins and is not quite as dry. The 1986 is even more of an improvement than the 1987 indicating that these wines have good aging potential. All are well balanced and should improve greatly for as much as ten years or more, and their reasonable

(1986) to moderate (1987 and 1988) price makes the wait worth while for those who have the proper storage.

Domaine Richeaume's Syrahs, vintages 1986 and 1988, contain 12.5 percent alcohol. Both are an opaque ruby with a medium body that is dry, oaky, and peppery with astringent tannins that give them a sharp taste. At least several years of aging should enhance these moderately priced wines.

Domaine Sainte-Anne, Entre-Deux-Mers from the Bordeaux region, vintage 1989, is an unclouded, medium purple-red with 11.5 percent alcohol. The appealing buttery and fruity scent is somewhat biting. This wine is very dry and medium bodied with a slightly round, full flavor. A marked acidity accompanies some tannins. With aging it could be a good wine and is one of the better French reds. The reasonable price encourages the wait.

Domaine Terres Blanches, Les Baux Rouge, vintage 1988, radiates a transparent, deep purple with 12 percent alcohol. The attractive, pleasant bouquet releases a positive fruity scent. This very dry, refreshing, medium- to full-bodied, moderately priced wine has good balance, but needs aging. It also comes in a 375-milliliter bottle that is high priced.

Guy Chaumont's Bourgogne Pinot Noir, vintage 1986, radiates a translucent pale to medium red with 12 percent alcohol. A woody, clean, and powerful bouquet identifies its Pinot Noir characteristics. The tart, medium-bodied flavor is offset by a marked level of tannins that would require more aging. Fairly balanced and moderately priced, this wine should improve with time. Those who desire a French wine with no added sulfites will find this Pinot Noir especially attractive.

Jean-Claude Rateau's Beaune Clos des Mariages, vintage 1988, contains 12.5 percent alcohol and is an opaque, medium purple-red. The pleasant and fruity scent complements the dry and medium-bodied taste with a marked acidity and a hint of stems. Aging will improve this fairly expensive wine.

French Rosés

Château Bousquette, Saint-Chinian Rosé, no vintage, is a transparent, pale red with 13 percent alcohol. The satisfying, alluring, and slightly fruity bouquet complements the dry, invigorating, and spicy light body that possesses good balance. Overall, it is attractive and reasonably priced.

Domaine de Torraccia, a 1989 vintage rosé, has 12 percent alcohol and sheds a pinkish amber. The aroma, slightly spicy with a hint of wild berry, matches the tart and stimulating flavor. As a good, fairly inexpensive rosé, it is a good value.

Domaine Richeaume rosés, vintages 1987 and 1989, have 12.5 percent alcohol. Both are a transparent pale red with a typical rosé bouquet that is sweet and fruity. They are dry, tart, and mild with a crisp punch flavor in a light body. The 1989 has a better fragrance and flavor than the 1987. These rosés are fairly well balanced and inexpensive (1987) to reasonably (1989) priced.

French Whites

Château Meric, Graves Blanc, vintage 1989, contains 12 percent alcohol and is a transparent pale yellow. The clean, pleasing aroma is matched with a dry to medium-dry, medium-bodied flavor that has a flat acidity. The good balance and moderate price make it a satisfactory sipping wine.

Domaine de Petit Roubié, Picpoul de Pinet, vintage 1990, has 11 percent alcohol. The transparent golden color accompanies an extremely mild bouquet and a watery, very light taste. The reasonable price is the most attractive attribute.

Domaine du Bourdieu, Entre-Deux-Mers, vintage 1989, contains 12 percent alcohol and radiates a transparent pale yellow. A clean, pleasing, and fruity fragrance combines well with a medium-dry, light- to medium-bodied flavor and a marked acidity. The good balance makes this a reasonably priced, decent table wine.

Domaine Richeaume, Cuvée, vintage 1986, has 12.5 percent alcohol. The transparent yellow is companion to an oak–pepper, mildly sharp bouquet. Astringent tannins offset the sharp, peppery, dry flavor. Fairly balanced, this wine is reasonably priced.

Guy Bossard's Muscadet de Sèvre-et-Maine contains 12 percent alcohol in its 1989 vintage. Radiating a transparent, pale yellow with a green tinge, its appealing, complex, fruity bouquet accompanies a dry, stimulating light body. This fine wine is moderately priced and should sell well.

Guy Chaumont's Bourgogne Blanc, Cépage Chardonnay, vintage 1989, has 12 percent alcohol. The pale yellow color matches the very mild scent and flat spectrum, semi-dry, acidic flavor. A reasonably moderate price and possible improvement with aging are the most attractive aspects.

Guy Chaumont's Givry Blanc, a white Burgundy Chardonnay, vintage 1988, sheds a lucid medium yellow. With an alcohol content of 12 percent, it provides an inviting vanilla-scented bouquet that is companion to a dry, invigorating, medium-bodied taste. This very well-balanced, choice wine is worth the high price.

Jean-Claude Rateau's Puligny-Montrachet, vintage 1988, contains 13 percent alcohol. A clear medium-gold Chardonnay, its appealing fruity essence complements the dry, refreshing, medium-bodied flavor that hints of rye. Consumers with expensive tastes will find this very well-balanced wine very enjoyable.

Jean Javillier's Meursault, vintage 1988, contains 12 percent alcohol and radiates a crystalline, medium pale yellow. The very appealing fruity essence matches the dry, enticing medium-bodied savor with a hint of almonds. Meursault is a well-balanced fine wine that is expensively priced but very enjoyable.

Jean Pierre Frick's Pinot Blanc, vintage 1989, has 12.5 percent alcohol. A pale, transparent yellow color accompanies an apple butter fragrance. Its medium-dry, luscious, flowery, mildly tart apple flavor hints of oak in an effervescent, medium body. The wine's good balance is enhanced by the reasonable price.

Jean Pierre Frick's Riesling, vintage 1989, contains 11.5 percent alcohol. This pale golden yellow, medium-bodied wine has an apple butter bouquet. The soft, mildly sweet, tart apple flavor is effervescent with a lasting tartness. As a fairly well-balanced wine, it sells at a moderate price.

Jean Pierre Frick's Gewürztraminer, vintage 1989, has an alcohol content of 13.5 percent, showing careful handling. A flowery, perfumed fruity essence comes from its pale, golden yellow hue.

Medium sweet to medium dry, this wine's savor is comrade to a refreshing, round, apple–pear, buttery, medium-light body. This is one of the best Gewürztraminers and the high price is worth it.

Jean Pierre Frick's Sylvaner, Vin d'Alsace, vintage 1989, contains 11.5 percent alcohol. The mild, fruity bouquet complements its light body that is dry, tart and refreshing. Mildly acidic, this pale, transparent yellow wine sells at a reasonable price.

Jean Pierre Frick's Chasselas, Vin d'Alsace, vintage 1990, contains 10.5 percent alcohol. A pale yellow color matches its very, very mild, buttery bouquet. The medium body accompanies a medium-dry, buttery flavor with a hint of rye. Fairly well balanced and fairly inexpensive, this wine makes an excellent choice for that special picnic.

La Coulée de Serrant, vintage 1986, has an alcohol content of 12 percent and radiates a pale golden yellow. The fragrance suggests smoke, yeast, and nitrogen. The flavor is full for a Chenin Blanc, with a gratifying fruity taste that hints of peaches and spice. The fairly good balance and expensive price make it a fairly good wine.

French Sparkling Wines and Champagne

Guy Bossard's Méthode Champenoise Brut, no vintage, has 12 percent alcohol. A transparent golden yellow matches a peachy essence that complements a light, clean, refreshing fruity savor. The high price is worthy of that special celebration which is enhanced by a sparkling wine.

Guy Bossard's Thuaud Vin Mousseux de Qualité, no vintage, is a very pale yellow at 12 percent alcohol. The nitrogenous and yeasty smell are a drawback to its dry, tart and generally uneven flavor. A fairly high price contributes to this wine's less than average rating.

Serge Faust's Champagne, Carte d'Or, no vintage, radiates a brilliant, star-bright, pale yellow with a light sparkle and contains 12 percent alcohol. The appealing, clean, and delightfully complex aroma emits a positive fruity fragrance. Dry (brut) with an enticing acidity and medium body, this very well-balanced, fine, true champagne is expensive but worth that special occasion. It is also available in 375-milliliter bottles.

German Reds

Sonnenbrunnen's Spätburgunder Rotwein Trocken from Baden, Germany, has no vintage and 12 percent alcohol. Translucent red with a medium bouquet, it comes across clean, fruity, and dry with a fruity aftertaste. This easy to drink wine with the potential to improve with age is a good value at a moderate price.

German Whites

Sonnenbrunnen's Müller-Thurgau Trocken, 1990 vintage, contains 11 percent alcohol. The transparent golden yellow has a peachy fragrance that matches the mildly peachy, bland medium body. The moderate price seems to make this wine worthwhile if it ages well.

Weingut Brüder Dr. Becker's Dienheimer Tafelstein Scheurebe Spätlese, vintage 1988, has 10 percent alcohol. The transparent golden yellow matches the mild bouquet. A peachy, medium-dry, well-balanced flavor has a dry finish. This is a fairly good wine and is reasonably priced.

Weingut Günter Wittman Rheinhessen, vintage 1988, has 12 percent alcohol. A transparent golden yellow is companion to an effervescent, tart, lemony savor that pleasantly lingers and then drops off. A fruity fragrance and very good balance are also appealing for a moderately priced white wine.

Italian Reds

La Suvera's Rango Rosso, vintage 1987, has an alcohol content of 12 percent and radiates a brilliant, medium ruby. A clean, slightly fruity bouquet complements a dry, invigorating, spicy, pungent, medium to light body. Its overall good balance and moderate price make it a good table wine.

Italian Whites

La Suvera's Bianco, vintage 1989, contains 11 percent alcohol. A clear pale yellow offers a clean, slightly fruity bouquet with a flat acidity and medium body. Thin and watery, it has a light, slightly grassy taste and a mild acidity. This wine possesses good balance and is moderately priced.

Steffano Bellotti's Gavi, vintage 1989, is a pale yellow with a 12 percent alcohol content. It is light bodied with a matching light, dry, slightly acidic taste that should be a good accompaniment to meals. The overall good balance and the moderate price make it an attractive wine.

Conclusion

In sum, the overall quality of these organic wines is impressive when compared with commercial wines: they were mostly good, a few were average with a potential to improve with age, and several were superior, in terms of body, acid–sugar balance, alcohol content, bouquet, and an overall sensual and gastronomical experience.[*] No doubt, the wines as a collection will get better. Equally important is that they were produced with the intent to preserve, protect, and enhance life on our planet. Most were produced by family-owned operations. These facts alone are reason enough to support them. They are preserving *our* environment and striving towards the highest quality standards for producing sound, healthy, delicious wine.

What is so surprising is that many of these high-quality wines are produced by wineries that have only been producing wines with organic grapes (and some use organic processing methods as well) for a short period of time; that is, within the past ten years. A number of them have only been exploring organic methods for the past couple of years. New techniques to produce wines without sulfites and other additives are continually being improved by a growing number of these pioneers. In sum, should organic wine be on your menu?—Unequivocally, yes!

If you are a wine connoisseur, or if you have never tried organic wine before, we encourage you to try these fruits of love's labor and see

---

[*] Several were undrinkable and were not included in these notes or the book.

for yourself what you are missing. And after you have done so, please let us know what you think, and we will pass on your comments to the wineries. Your comments will greatly be appreciated. Please write to the Organic Connection, Post Office Box 88, Tempe, Arizona 85280. Also indicate if you would like to be notified as to future revised editions of the *Consumer's Guide to Organic Wines*. May peace, love, and optimal health be yours.

Bibliography

A Survey of Wine Service in Hospitals in the Top Metropolitan Areas of the United States. (1985). San Francisco: Matheson and Matheson.

60 Minutes. (1991). "The French Paradox" [French high fat diet and corresponding low heart attack rate primarily attributed to consumption of wine]. *60 Minutes* (Nov. 17), 51 West 52nd St., 34th Floor, N.Y., N.Y. 10019.

Academic American Encyclopedia. (1990). Danbury, Conn.: Grolier Publishers.

Adams, P. (1987). *The Wine Lover's Quiz Book*. London: Rainbird Publishing Group, Ltd.

Allaway, W. H. (1975). *Effect of Soils and Fertilizers on Human and Animal Nutrition*. Agriculture Information Bulletin No. 378, Washington, D.C., USGPO.

Amerine, M. A. (1986). *Bibliography of Publications by the Faculty, Staff, and Students of the University of California, 1876–1980, on Grapes, Wines, and Related Subjects*. Berkeley: University of California Press.

Amerine, M. A., and C. S. Ough. (1974). *Wine and Must Analysis*. New York: John Wiley & Sons.

Amerine, M. A., et al. (1972). *Technology of Wine Making*. Westport, Conn.: Avi Publishing Company. (see also later editions)

Arizona Tribune. (1991). "Wine Industry Promotes Product as Health Food." *Arizona Tribune* (Phoenix) June 23:A9.

Asinof, L. (1989). "Business Bulletin: A Special Background Report on Trends in Industry and Finance. Wine Without Sniffles" [Frey Vineyards]. *Wall Street Journal* March 2:1.

Bagley, R. (1981). "Diet and Behavioral Problems. *Journal of Orthomolecular Psychiatry* 10:284–298.

Bailey, A. (1991). "Winery Takes Pride in Their Product [Ponderosa Vineyards]." *Lebanon Express* (Lebanon, Oreg.) August 21:1.

Balzer, R. L. (1984). "Don't Say 'No' to Paul Thomas Crimson Rhubarb." *Los Angeles Times Home* September 16:28–30.

Balzer, R. L. (1986). "From Rhubarb to Riesling: A '60s Rebel Becomes a Force in Washington State Wines" [Paul Thomas]. *Los Angeles Times* November 23:30.

131

Barrett, J. T. (1990). "California's Rhône?: Haas, Beaucastel Owners in Venture." *Wine Spectator* May 15:13.

Beadle, P. (1978). *Brew It Yourself: A Complete Guide to the Making of Wine, Liquors, and Soft Drinks,* 3rd revised edition. New York: Farrar, Straus & Giroux.

Beleme, J. (1990). "Wine: The Organic Alternative." *EastWest* 20(5):82–89.

Berger, D. E., and J. R. Snortum. (1989). "Alcoholic Beverage Preferences of Drinking–Driving Violators." *Journal of Studies on Alcohol* 46(3):232-239.

Bittman, M. (1991). "Organic French Wines Rise in Quality, Value." *Hartford Courant* (Harford, Conn.) June 19:E7.

Borg, S., et al. (1987). "Alcohol Consumption, Dependence, and Central Norepinephrine Metabolism in Humans." Pages 181–190 in J. Engel, et al., editors. *Brain Reward Systems and Abuse.* New York: Raven Press.

Bouthyette, P., et al. (1989). "Wine and Beer Making for Liberal Arts Science Education." *Journal of College Science Teaching* 19(2):84–90.

Bowden, S. C. (1987). "Brain Impairment in Social Drinkers? No Cause for Concern." *Alcoholism: Clinical and Experimental Research* 11:407–410.

Briseno, O. (1989). "Wrath of Grapes." *San Diego Union* April 26:E1,E3.

Bullard, R. (1991). "Much Ado about Lead: FDA Seeks Standards for Wine." *Wine Spectator* July 31:8.

California Organic Foods Act of 1990 (AB2012). Pages A1–A10 in *California Certified Organic Farmers 1991 Certification Handbook.* Santa Cruz: California Certified Organic Farmers.

Canali, L. (1991). "Fruit of the Vine: Is there such a Thing as Organic Wine?" *OFPANA Reports: Newsletter of the Organic Foods Production Assocation of North America* (Greenfield, Mass.) November:1.

Canton, C. (1989). "Rhubarb Wine Put Paul Thomas on Map." *Journal American: The Eastside's Community Newspaper* (Bellevue, Wash.) October 30:C1.

Chambers, K. (1988). "Wine Drinkers Have Some Organic Options" [Frey Vineyards]. *Register-Guard* (Eugene, Oreg.) November 10.

Chartrand, P. (1992). "Pioneers in the Organic Wine Industry." *In Business* 14(1):24.

Chen, Y., and Y. Avnimelech, editors. (1986). *Role of Organic Matter in Modern Agriculture*. Boston: Martinus Nijhoff.

Chroman, N. (1983). "Bonanza of Dry-Fruit Table Wines: Paul Thomas Overcomes a Universal Bias for Grapes." *Los Angeles Times* June 2, Part VIII:32,36.

Clarke, O. (1985). *The Essential Wine Book: A Guide to Appreciating and Enjoying the Wines of the World*. New York: Viking Penguin.

Clifford, W. (1990). "Vintners Returning to Organic Farming." *Washington Times* July 18:F3.

Clifford, W. (1991). "Organic Wines to Grow in Number, Popularity." *Washington Times* July 31:F2.

Cowen, R. (1989). "Chromium May Prevent Type II Diabetes Onset." *Science News* 137:214.

Cox, J. (1992). "Red, White and You: A Healthy Man's Guide to Wine." *Men's Health* August:82–85.

Dahl, R., et al. (1986). "Red Wine Asthma." *Journal of Allergy and Clinical Immunology* 78:1126–1129.

Deveny, K. (1991). "Wine Makers Criticize Study Showing High Levels of Lead in Their Products." *Wall Street Journal* August 2:B4,B8.

Engeman, R. M., and L. G. Pank. (1984). "Potential Secondary Toxicity From Anticoagulant Pesticides Contaminating Human Food Sources." *New England Journal of Medicine* 311:257–258.

Figiel, R. (1989). "Back to the Future: Organic Viniculture—From California's Fetzer to the Rhône Valley's Château Beaucastel." *International Wine Review* October–November:8–14.

Fisher, L. M. (1991). "Organic Wine Enters the Mainstream." *New York Times* November 19:D1,D6.

Fisher, L. M. (1992). "Organic Wines Enter Mainstream." *In Business* 14(1):22.

Flynn, M., et al. (1989). "Holiday Spirits." *Geriatric Nursing* 10(6):292–293.

Ford, G. (1988). *Benefits of Moderate Drinking*. San Francisco: Wine Appreciation Guild.

Forkner, D. J. (1982). "Should Wine Be on Your Menu?" *Professional Nutritionist* Spring:1–3.

Forkner, D. J. (1984). "Your Key to a Healthy Heart." *Vintage Magazine* November:9–13.

Forrest, F., et al. (1991). "Reported Social Alcohol Consumption During Pregnancy and Infants' Development at 18 Months." *British Medical Journal* 303(6793):22–26.

Fowles, G. (1989). "The Complete Home Wine-Maker" *New Scientist* 123(1680):38–45.

Freidman, L. A., and A. W. Kimball. (1986). "Coronary Heart Disease Mortality and Alcohol Consumption in Framingham. *American Journal of Epidemiology* 124:481–489.

Friss, D. (1989). "Organic Wines:Avoiding 80 Additives." *Longevity* July:74–75.

George, R. (1989). "Greener Than Thou" [Includes organic French wine tasting results]. *Wine* (Teddington, Midox, England) August:69–74.

Gleave, D. (1988). "Organic Wines: Fad and Fantasy?" *Wine* December:49–52.

Gordon T., and W. B. Kannel. (1984). "Drinking and Mortality. The Framingham Study." *American Journal of Epidemology* 120:97–107.

Grape Press. (1991). "Topolos at Russian River Vineyards." *Grape Press* (Fulton, Calif.) April:1–2.

Grossman, H. J. (1974). *Grossman's Guide to Wines, Spirits and Beers.* New York: Charles Scribner's Sons.

Gunn, J., and D. F. Farrington, editors. (1982). *Abnormal Offenders, Delinquency and the Criminal Justice System.* New York: Van Nostrand–Reinhold.

Guralnik, J. M., and G. A. Kaplan. (1989). "Predictors of Healthy Aging: Prospective Evidence from Alameda County Study." *American Journal of Public Health* 79(6):705.

Hippchen, L. J. (1976). *Ecologic-Biochemical Approaches to Treatment of Delinquents and Criminals.* New York: Van Nostrand–Reinhold.

Hippchen, L. J., editor. (1982). *Holistic Approach to Offender Rehabilitation.* Springfield, Ill.: Charles C. Thomas.

Hoffmeister, F., and G. Stille, editors. (1982). *Handbook of Experimental Pharmacology, Volume 55/III, Psychotropic Agents, Part III: Alcohol and Psychotomimetics. Psychotropic Effects of Central Acting Drugs.* New York: Springer–Verlag.

Johnson, H. (1977). *The World Atlas of Wine: The Classic Guide to the Wines and Spirits of the World*. New York: Simon & Schuster.

Joseph, R. (1985). "A Natural High." *New Health* October:63–64.

Kastenbaum, R. (1988). "In Moderation." *Generations* Summer:71.

Kastenbaum, R., and B. Mishara. (1980). *Alcohol and Old Age*. New York: Grune & Stratton.

Klatsky, A. L., et al. (1981). "Alcohol and Mortality: A Ten-Year Kaiser Permanente Experience." *Annals of Internal Medicine* 95(2):139–145.

Kutsky, R. J. (1982). *Handbook of Vitamins, Minerals and Hormones*. New York: Van Nostrand–Reinhold.

Land, L. (1988). "Small Matters: Organically Grown Wine." *American Wine & Food: The American Institute of Wine & Food Monthly* October:9–10.

LaPorte, R., et al. (1985). "Alcohol, Coronary Heart Disease, and Total Mortality." *Recent Developments in Alcoholism* 3:161.

LaRaia, A. (1989). "The Urethane Question." *Wine Times* November:48.

Lawther, J. (1991). "France's Natural Move to Organic Wine." *Wine Spectator* November:125–126.

Leighton, T. (1989). Paper presented at the Symposium on Carcinogens, Mutagens, and Anti-Carcinogenic Factors in Foods at the American Chemical Society's Meeting, Dallas, April 9–14. *Berkeley Press Release* No. 11270:1–2.

Lichine, A. (1977). *Alexis Lichine's New Encyclopedia of Wines and Spirits*. New York: Alfred A. Knopf.

Living Earth: Journal of the Soil Association. (1989). "On the Market: Francis Blake Looks at the Organic Food Awards and the Organic Wine Fair." *The Living Earth: Journal of the Soil Association* October 1:22–23.

Longevity. (1989). "A Practical Guide to the Art and Science of Staying Young." *Longevity* 1(10).

Lucia, S. (1963). *History of Wine as Therapy*. Philadelphia, Pa.: J. B. Lippincott.

Lucia, S., editor. (1969). *Wine and Health*. San Francisco: Fortune House.

Lucia, S. (1971). *Wine and Your Well-being*. New York: Popular Library.

Lucia, S. (1972). "Wine: A Food Throughout The Ages." *American Journal of Clinical Nutrition* 25:361,372.

Lynch, K. (1988). *Adventures on the Wine Route: A Wine Buyer's Tour of France*. New York: Farrar, Straus & Giroux.

MacNeil, K. (1990). "Growing Organic Awareness in Mendocino." *Wine Spectator* February 28:41–43.

Mansson, P.-H. (1989). "The Hess Collection" [Special Reprint Edition]. *Wine Spectator* September 30:33–35.

Mansson, P.-H. (1991). "New Study Finds Pregnant Women Can Imbibe Safely." *Wine Spectator* August 31:11.

Mariani, J. (1990). "I'll Have What Dad Had." *Esquire* September:66.

Marquez, T. (1991). "On the Organic Trail." *OFPANA Reports: Newsletter of the Organic Foods Production Association of North America* November:6.

Matthews, T. (1989). "Cosmic Rhythms in the Loire" [La Coulée de Serrant]. *Wine Spectator* February 15:48.

Matthews, T. (1991). "Top German Estates Ban Herbicide Use." *Wine Spectator* July 31:8.

McConnell, M. (1987). *Mediterranean Diet*. New York: W. W. Norton.

McDonald, J. (1982). "Nutritional Aspects of Wine Consumption." *Urban Health* March:23.

Macdonough, G. (1990). "Hot Little Numbers" [Domaine de Trévallon]. *Wine* (Teddington, Midox, England) May:68–69.

Mead, J. (1988). "Topolos: Wine That's Different." *Sacramento Union* June 30:C19,C20.

Mendelson, J., et al. (1982). "Hospital Treatment of Alcoholism: A Profile of Middle Income Americans." *Alcoholism: Clinical and Experimental Research* 6(3):379.

Mitchell, C., and M. Jacobson. (1987). *Chemical Additives in Booze*. Washington, D.C.: Center for Science in the Public Interest.

National Department of Justice, Bureau of Justic Statistics. (1988). "Special Report." Page 1.

New Health. (1985). "A Natural High." *New Health* October:63–64.

OGWA (Organic Grapes into Wine Alliance) Newsletter. 1991. Spring–Summer:2.

Ouch, C. S., and M. A. Amerine. (1988). *Methods for Analysis of Musts and Wines*. New York: John Wiley & Sons.

Paoli, R. (1987). "Wines for the Pope's San Francisco Supper." *Epicure* September 9:3.

PCC Sound Consumer. (1987). "Paul Thomas Crimson Rhubarb Wine Contains No Sulfites." *PCC Sound Consumer* September:2.

Pearce, F. (1987). "Pesticide Deaths: The Price of the Green Revolution." *New Scientist* 114(1565):30.

Pittman, D. J., and H. Klein. (1989). "Perceived Consequences Associated with the Use of Beer, Wine, Distilled Spirits, and Wine Coolers." *International Journal of Addiction* 25:471-494.

Prial, F. J. (1988). "You Can't Tell a Wine's Sulfites Even With Labels." *New York Times* April 13:C1,C14.

Prial, F. J. (1990). "Wine Talk: Rowdy and Chucky Drive an Ecology-Oriented Cultivation of Wine Grapes in Sonoma County" [Bellerose Vineyard]. *New York Times* January 31:C12:3.

Remond, A., and C. Izard, editors. (1979). *Electrophysiological Effects of Nicotine.* New York: Elsevier/North–Holland.

Renaud, S. and M. de Lorgeril. (1992). "Wine Alcohol Platelets, and the French Paradox for Coronary Heart Disease." *Lancet* 339:1523-1526.

Rich, L. (1991). "Natural Wines Exude Sophisticated Taste." *Sun-Sentinel* (Miami, Florida) May 9:9.

Rieger, T. (1989). "Organic Commitment Pays Off for Frey Vineyards." *Vineyard & Winery Management* September–October:36–41.

Roby, N. (1988). "Top-Notch Organic Red Wines." *Wine Spectator* February 15:12.

Rosett, H. and L. Weiner. (1984). *Alcohol and the Fetus.* New York: Oxford University Press.

Ryweck, J. (1982). "Paul Thomas: A Wine of the Country." *Puget Consumers' Co-op Newsletter* (Seattle, Wash.) February:8.

Schauss, A. G. (1978). *Orthomolecular Treatment of Criminal Offenders.* Berkeley, Calif.: Michael Lesser M.D.

Schauss, A. G. (1980). *Diet, Crime and Delinquency.* Berkeley, Calif.: Parker House.

Schauss, A. G. (1983). "Nutrition and Behavior." *Journal of Applied Nutrition* 35:30–43.

Schauss, A. G., and C. Simonsen. (1979). "Critical Analysis of the Diets of Chronic Juvenille Offenders, Part I." *Journal of Orthomolecular Psychiatry* 8:30–43.

Schoonmaker, F. (1978). *Frank Schoonmaker's Encyclopedia of Wine,* revised and expanded by J. Wile. New York: Hastings House.

Schuphan, W. (1974). "Nutritional Value of Crops as Influenced by Organic and Inorganic Fertilizer Treatments." *Quality of Plants and Plant Foods in Human Nutrition* 23:333–358.

Scolionkov, D. (1989). "The Marriage of Wine and Food-Finding Wines for Today's Lighter, Healthier Dishes." *American Health* 8(9):66.

Shaper, A. G., et al. (1988). "Alcohol and Mortality in British Men: Explaining the U-Shaped Curve." *Lancet* 2:1267–1273.

Smith, R. (1989). "The Organic Revolution." *San Francisco Chronicle* (Marin–Sonoma Edition) April 26:Food 1,9.

Sousanis, M. (1990). "Greek Hospitality: Topolos Winery and Restaurant." *Bayfood: The Bay Area's Guide to Cooking and Dining* (San Francisco) April.

St. Leger, A., and A. L. Cochrane. (1979). Factors Associated with Cardiac Mortality in Developed Countries with Particular Reference to the Consumption of Wine. *Lancet* I:1017-1020.

Steiman, H. (1989). "Washington's Maverick Vintner: Paul Thomas" [Cover Story]. *Wine Spectator* October 15:28.

Stockley, T. (1990). "Organically Grown Wines are Taste Treat, Too." *Seattle Times* March 7:C1,C7.

Street, R. (1989). "Cultivating a Niche for Organic Wine." *Wine Spectator* February 28:37–39.

Street, R. (1990). "The True Believers" [Frey Vineyards]. *San Jose Mercury News, West* October 14:8–13.

Street, R. (1990). "Going Organic in California." *Wine Spectator* September 30:54–63.

Street, R. (1990). "Vintners Disagree Over What Organic Means." *Wine Spectator* September 30:58–60.

Street, R. (1991). "Breaking Tradition: Mendocino County Emerges as the Leader in Organic Wine Production." *California Farmer* January 5:10,51,53.

Street, R. (1992). "Breaking with Tradition." [Orleans Hill Winery] *Practical Winery* March–April:32.

Streissguth, A. P., et al. (1990). "Moderate Prenatal Alcohol Exposure Effects on Child IQ and Learning Problems at Age 7 1/2 Years Old." *Alcohol: Clinical and Experimental Research* 14(5):662–669.

Sugarman, C. (1988). "FDA Won't Extend Ban on Sulfites in Food." *Washington Post* July 20:A3.

Thomases, D. (1991). "Gamble Pays Off in Provence" [Domaine de Trevallon]. *Wine Spectator* November 15:132–133.

Thompson, S. (1989). "The Pleasure Principle: The Best Prescription for a Long and Healthy Life Could Be a Little Red Wine, A Good Novel, and a Daily Nap." *Health* 21(8):28–30.

Tsevat, J., et al. (1987). "Fatal Asthma After Ingestion of Sulfite-Containing Wine." *Annals of Internal Medicine* 107:263.

Underground Wine Journal. (1990). "Best Buy" [Topolos at Russian River Vineyards]. June:265.

Van Thiel, D. H., and R. Lester. (1976). Alcoholism: Its Effect on Hypothalamic, Pituitary Gonadal Function. *Gastroenterology* 71:318–327.

Vincent, G. (1990). "Topolos is Winemaker, Grapegrower, Educator." *NorthCoast, The Farmer* (San Francisco) April 18:2.

Vineyard & Winery Management. (1989). "Entrepreneur Imports French Organic Wines" [Organic Wine Company]. September–October:38.

Vineyard & Winery Management. (1989). "Organic Standards: BYO." September–October:41.

Walker, L. (1988). "California Wines Are Going Organic" [Frey Vineyards]. *San Francisco Chronicle* October 26.

Walker, L. (1990). "A Look at California Nouveau." *San Francisco Chronicle* November 20.

Walpole I., et al. (1991). "Low to Moderate Maternal Alcohol Use Before and During Pregnancy, and Neurobehavioral Outcome in the Newborn Infant." *Developmental Medicine and Child Neurology* 33(10):875-883.

Washington Post. (1987). "Grapes Must Be Free of Sulfites by Jan. 1." *Washington Post* December 30:A14.

Woehler, R. (1992). "Japan's Taste for Premium Wine Leads to Washington's Finest." [Badger Mountain Vineyard] *Tri-City Herald* (Pasco, Kennewick, and Richland, Wash.) February 20:C1.

Woehler, R. (1990). "Grape Grower Turns Winemaker with an Organic Twist" [Badger Mountain Vineyard]. *Tri-City Hearld* (Pasco, Kennewick, and Richland, Wash.) January 24:C1.

World Health Organization. (1989). *Lead—Environmental Aspects*. Geneva: World Health Organization.

World Health Organization. (1978). *Alcohol-Related Problems: The Need to Develop Further the WHO Initiative*. November 27. Report Director General, WHO Document EP 63/23. Geneva: World Health Organization.

Wurtman, R. J., and J. D. Fernstrom. (1974). "Effects of the Diet on Brain Neurotransmitters." *Nutrition Reviews* 32:193–200.

Wurtman, R. J., and J. J. Wurtman, editors. (1977–1985). *Nutrition and the Brain*. New York: Raven Press.

Index

A

à Notre Mer 119
à Notre Terre 56
Abakanowicz, Magdalena 58
acacia wood 86. *See also* casks
Academic American Encyclopedia 21
acetum 21
achillea 96
acid xi, 22, 46, 49, 128; acetic 22; amino
1, 24; strength of 21; tannic 22. *See
also* pH; tannins
acidification 14
acidity 5, 17, 21, 22
acids 48
addiction. *See* alcoholism; eating disorders
additives xi, xii, 4, 13, 17, 20, 49, 63, 75,
76, 103, 128; chemical 106. *See also
Chemical Additives in Booze*
adrenal glands 2
Adventures on the Wine Route 86
advertising standards 38
affidavit 12
aggressiveness 3
aging 5, 22, 24, 50, 63, 67
agitating 100
agriculture xii, 38, 41, 44, 82, 83, 102;
conventional xi, 11, 16, 98;
sustainable 66
Albarello 50, 112
alcohol ix, 1, 3, 4, 5, 20, 21, 22, 23, 27,
29, 31, 32, 34, 35, 36, 38, 70, 101, 103;
abuse 2, 29; content 22, 26, 33,
34, 72, 128; ethyl 23; use 26
Alcohol and Old Age 31
alcoholic *See* alcohol; alcoholism
Alcoholic Beverage Labeling Act 26
alcoholic beverages 6, 10, 26, 32, 36
alcoholism 1, 6, 29, 30
*Alcoholism: Clinical and Experimental
Research* 29
Alicante-Bouschet 77, 78, 113
Allah 32
allergic xi, 17, 54, highly 17; reactions 17,
54. *See also* sulfites: allergic reactions to
Alsace 25, 85
Alsatian: grape varieties 103; wines 55
America 38

American 132; artists 58; Chardonnays
82; clinicians 3; consumers 92;
cooking 84; health 138; oak barrels
60, 64; organic wine 41; processing
equipment 43; wine xiii
American Medical Association 31
American Wine Alliance for Research and
Education (AWARE) 36
Americans xi, 29, 31
Americans for Safer Beverages 36
Amerine, M. A. 21, 22, 24, 25
amines 21
amino acids. *See* acid: amino
Amity, Oregon 42
ancient history 158
ancient method 47
Anderson Valley 47, 66
André Chaumont 83, 120
André Stentz 20, 85
Angelica 34
Angola 4
animal 11; products xi
Anjou 90, 95
annual farm visit 13
anorexia 3, 6
antidiuretic hormone. *See* ADH (antidiuretic
hormone)
antifreeze 4. *See also* additives
antioxidant 5, 20, 24, 45. *See also* additives
antiseptic 5, 32
anxiety: reducing 6
apertifs 34, 85
Apgar, Aleta 63
appellation 83; Châteauneauf-du-Pape 95;
Côtes du Rhône 95; Wild Horse Valley
46. *See also* Appellation Contrôlée
Appellation Contrôlée 46, 83, 87, 89, 90,
91, 92, 97, 99
Appellation d'Origine Contrôlée. *See*
Appellation Contrôlée
appetizer wines 33, 34, 35. *See also* apertifs
Argentina 4
Arizona 37, 78, 85, 92, 103, 158
aroma 44, 47, 58, 68, 69, 77, 85, 87, 93, 95
art exhibits 58. *See also* Hess Collection, The
arteriosclerosis ix. *See also* heart disease
ascorbic acid. *See* vitamin: C
ash 23. *See also* sulfites
Association of German Prädikatswein
Estates 100

Association of Organic Wine Growers in
    Rheinhessen 100
asthma x, 4, 5, 24; fatal 18
audit trail 12
Auslese 101
Australia 51
authorities. *See* expert
award 65. *See also* award-winning: wines
award, bronze medal 69; Pinot Noir 72;
    Zinfandel 69
award, gold medal 60, 61, 65, 68, 77;
    Alicante-Bouschet 77, 78; Petite Sirah
    78; Reisling 60; Zinfandel 69, 79
award, silver medal 68; Cabernet Sauvignon
    67; red 72; Syrah 55; Zinfandel 60
award-winning: as identifying quality 25;
    Charbono 76; wines 53, 57, 60, 68, 69

B

B-complex. *See* vitamin: B-complex
Bacon, Francis 58, 59
bacteria 49, 86
Baden 127
Badger Mountain 43
Badger Mountain Vineyard and Winery 43,
    80, 114, 115, 116, 118, 119, 140
balance: biochemical 29; brain-chemical 2,
    24; hormone 1; in nature 11; mineral
    8; of light 35; of microecology 5, 22;
    of wine xi, 20, 43, 44, 46, 47, 49, 58,
    60, 66, 67, 78, 79, 96, 97
Banner Mountain Vineyard 64, 65
Barbera 33, 55, 56, 113
Bartlett pear wine 69
Baselitz, Georg 58
bases. *See* additives
BATF 18, 28, 42, 46, 49, 70
Bay Area 76
Beaucastel 95, 132
Beaujolais 33, 69, 87
Beaujolais Nouveau 87
Beaune Clos des Mariages 123
Beaune red 83
Bechtheimer Hasensprung Huxelrebe
    Spätlese 101
beer x, 2, 3; violence and 3
Beerenauslese 101
Belgian draft horses 44
Belgium 4
Bellerose Vineyard 44, 80, 107, 109, 117,
beneficial: effects of wine ix, x, 30, 37, 10;
    effects of the sun 102; insects 77, 105;
    organisms 11, 49; predators 49
Benefits of Moderate Drinking ix

Bergamini, Marquis Ricci Paracciani 93
Berjerac 89, 90
Bianco 128
Bible 32
bing cherry wine 69
Bio-Dynamic Farming and Gardening
    Association 16, 36
Bio-System™, The 49
biochemistry 1, 2
biodegradable 56
biodynamic 13, 36, 94, 102; compounds
    96; methods 96
biodynamically grown 16
birth defects 27
bisulfite 61. *See also* metabisulfites;
    potassium: bisulfite; potassium:
    metabisulfite; sulfites
Blanc de Noir 52
blood xi; pressure patterns 31; vessels
    1, 2
blood sugar problems. *See* diabetes
blooming. *See* flowering cycle
Blue Heron Block 51
Blue Heron Lake Winery 46, 80, 115
blush wine 44, 114. *See also* rosé wine
body 128, 158; image 3
Bordeaux 81, 82, 89, 123; Blanc 92;
    blends 44; mixture 96
Bossard, Guy. *See* Guy Bossard
botrytes 63, 111. *See also* late harvested; rot
bottling practices 14
bouillie bordelaise 97
bouquet 47, 82, 95, 97, 103, 128. *See also*
    tasting: notes
Bourboulenc 94
Bourgogne: Blanc 125; Chardonnay 82;
    Pinot Noir 82, 123
Bousquette. *See* Château Bousquette
boycotts xi
brain-chemicals 4, 24
brandy 72
bread 35
breath: shortness of 72
breathe 24
Briceland Vineyards 47, 80, 108, 109, 115,
    116, 117, 120
British Medical Journal 30
brix. *See* sugar
bronze medal. *See* award, bronze medal
browning 61
Brut méthode champenoise. *See* champagne;
    méthode champenoise
bubbles 35
Buena Vista Winery xi
bulimia 6

Bundökologischer Weinhau 100
Burgundy 25, 83; region of 48, 82
Butte County 61, 63

C

Cabernet Franc 45, 90
Cabernet Sauvignon 33, 44, 45, 47, 50, 51,
   52, 54, 57, 58, 63, 64, 67, 74, 75, 76,
   82, 90, 93, 98, 99, 107; blend 88;
   grapes 62, 99
Cabernet varieties 69
calcium 2, 31, 96
California xii, 13, 28, 36, 37, 39, 42, 49,
   51, 65, 67, 76, 78, 79, 89, 92, 103;
   Northern 61; coastal valley 66; ports
   73
California Action Network (CAN) 38
California Certified Organic Farmers Associa-
   tion 13, 39, 46, 47, 50, 51, 52, 54, 55,
   58, 60, 68; 1991 Certification Handbook
   39
California Department of Food and Agriculture
   xi
California Department of Health Services 19
California Grapevine 47
California Health and Safety Code 12
California Organic Foods Act of 1990 11,
   12, 13, 39, 45, 54, 61
California Organic Wine Alliance. See Organic
   Grapes into Wine Alliance
California Pacific Medical Center 30
California State Fair 69
California Wine Institute 28
Calistoga, California 74
calming effect 3
calories 3
Cameron Winery 48, 110
Canada 78
Canaiolo 93
cancer 86. See cardiovascular diseases
candida 3, 4
carbohydrates 4
carbon dioxide 68
cardiac: death x, 9; health 2
cardiovascular: diseases 2; survival ix
Carignane 33, 54, 90, 112
Carneros 46
Carte d'Or 126
casein xi
casks 17; oak 93, 103; steel 22;
   wooden 86, 100
casseroles 84
catalysts 4. See also additives
cathecholamines 4. See also brain-chemicals

Cattrall Brothers Vineyard 42, 48
CCOF. See California Certified Organic
   Farmers Association
cellars 100
cellulose filtration 103
Center for Science in the Public Interest x, 36
central nervous system 2
Central Valley 66; vineyards xi
centrifuges 102. See also pumps: centrifugal
Cepage Chardonnay 125
certification 11, 36
certified: organic xii, 14, 46, 47, 49, 51, 81,
   83, 85, 90, 91, 92; organically grown
   12, 16, 42, 52, 55, 56, 60, 66, 72, 76,
   77, 99; and processed 13, 48
certifying organization 15; private 13
chamomile 96
champagne 14, 85, 89; about 35. See also
   méthode champenoise
chaptalization 101, 103. See also Paul
   Thomas Winery
Chapter 15.86 Revised Code (Washington) 12
Charbono 33, 75, 76, 113
Chardonnay 33, 44, 46, 47, 51, 56, 57, 58,
   60, 61, 65, 66, 74, 77, 82, 83, 85, 115;
   barrel-fermented 43; oak-aged 44;
   sparkler 77
Chartrand Imports 21, 81
Chartrand, Paul 81
Chasselas 126
Château Bousquette 83, 91, 120, 124
Château de Beaucastel 94, 95, 120;
   Blanc 94
Château du Moulin de Peyronin 81, 121
Château la Maubastit 89, 121
Château Meric 15, 81, 121, 124
Chateau Ste. Michelle 43
Châteauneuf-du-Pape 25, 87, 94, 95
Chaumont, Guy. See Guy Chaumont
Chaumont Vineyard 82
Chavez, Cezar xi
Chemical Additives in Booze 36
Chemical Society x
chemical-free ix, x
chemicals: synthetic 14, 98. See also
   additives: chemical; agricultural. See
   fertilizers: chemical
Chenin Blanc 33, 51, 96; grape 95
chicken 28; and wine 33; egg 20. See
   also sulfites
Chico 61
children 30, 50, 71, 73
cholesterol ix, 2; beneficial types of ix.
   See also acids
Christian Brothers 57

143

Christian Ducroux 87, 121
chromium 2, 3. *See also* minerals
Cigliegiolo 93
Cinsault 88, 94, 97
Clairette 94
clarification 14, 60, 100
classification of organic wineries 80
classical vinification 95
cleaning methods 14. *See also* sterilization
    methods
clear and reasonable warning 28
Clifford, William 85
climate 84; conditions 20; dessert 43;
    micro- 52, 76
clonal breeding 96
clone-type vinestocks 16
Clos des Mariages 83
coal burning 28
cold processing 16
cold stabilization 60
Colfax 64
collage 16
collagen xi
Coloma Canyon Vineyard 52
color 47, 68, 77, 79, 88, 95. *See also*
    tasting: notes
Colorado 78, 92
coloring agents 14
Columbia River Valley 43
complex ix, 4, 16, 48, 52, 58, 60, 61, 68,
    69, 73, 76, 95
compost 16, 62, 66, 71, 96, 102
confirmation 12
congeners 5
Connecticut 78
consumer x; opinions 25; practices xii,
    105
consumerism xii, 65
consumption 2; moderate 30
containers: temperature-controlled 88
Contains Sulfites 70
copper sprays 17, 100. *See also* chemicals:
    synthetic; fungicides; sulfur
corks 14, 28, 35
Cornell University xi
coronary disease. *See* heart disease: coronary
Corsica 97
Corvée des Vignes 83
cosmic rhythms. *See* biodynamic; *Cycles
    Magazine*; Zodiac constellations
Côte de Beaune 83
Coteaux d'Aix-en-Provence 98, 122
Coteaux du Layon 90
Coteaux Varois 87, 122

Côtes de Provence 99
Côtes du Rhône 25, 87, 92, 95, 122
Coturri and Sons, H. 49, 80, 108, 110, 111,
    112
Coturri, Tony 49
Coudoulet de Beaucastel 95, 121
Counoise 94
cover crop 49, 57, 66, 67. *See also* legumes
cramps 17. *See also* sulfites: allergic reactions
    to
cream sherry 34. *See also* dessert wines
credible source 12
crime statistics 3
Crimson Rhubarb 69, 114
critic. *See* expert
crop dusters 28
crop yield 100
cru 97
cru Chablis 47
cultivating 71
culture biologique 14
cultured drinks 6
cuvée: Bellerose Cabernet Sauvignon 45,
    107; Domaine Richeaume 99, 124; Jean
    Pierre Frick 103; Roussanne 95
cycles 158
Cycles Magazine 158

D

Dallas x
dampness. *See* storage: proper
dark foods 33
deaths xi, 17; among farm workers xi
decant 24, 72, 93
deformities xi
Defrauders 32
deionized water 1
Demeter 13, 16, 91, 102. *See also*
    biodynamic
Demeter Association, The 16, 36
demonstrations xi
Dennison Brothers 47
Dennison, Peter 66
Dennison Vineyards 66
Dennison, Will 66
dependence: problems 29
depression 6
dessert wines 3, 22, 23, 33, 34, 72; serving
    temperature of 34
deterioration 17
Deuteronomy 32
diabetes 6; mellitus 3, 23
Dictionary of American Wine xiii

144

Dienheimer Tafelstein Scheurebe *Spätlese* 101, 127
diets 3, 4, 6
digestion 5
digestive system cancers 6. *See also* candida; disease; intestinal cancers
disease 6, 158
disease-preventive 2
distilled: liquor 27; spirits 3
distributors: U.S. ix
diuretic 1
doctors 2
domaine 97
Domaine de la Bousquette. *See* Château Bousquette
Domaine de la Gautière 87, 121
Domaine de la Jasse 87, 122
Domaine de Petit Roubié 84, 124
Domaine de Tavernel 90, 122
Domaine de Torraccia 124
Domaine de Trévallon 88, 94, 98, 122
Domaine des Cedres 83, 84, 122
Domaine du Bas Deffens 86, 122
Domaine du Bourdieu 82, 124
Domaine du Daumas Gassac 88, 121
Domaine Richeaume 99, 122, 123, 124
Domaine Sainte-Anne 82, 123
Domaine Terres Blanches 84, 123
Domaine Torraccia 97
domestic 28
drinking xii; moderate ix, 1, 6, 30, 31, 32, 38. *See also* alcoholism
drought resistant 105
drugs 29
Dry Creek Valley 44
dry farming 28, 29, 71, 73, 77
Dürrbach, Aloi 98

E

Earth 16, 56, 89, 96, 158
East Coast 41, 60
eating disorders 6, 29
Ecclesiastes 32
Eco-Wine 42
economic xii, xiii, 38, 51, 67, 75, 106
ecosystem(s) 77, 105
Eddy, Rusty xiii
education xiii, 26, 36, 37, 89, 92, 157
egg: white xi; yolk 20, 23. *See also* chicken: egg
Eire Ban 52, 117
El Dorado Barbera 55, 113
elderly 3, 31
Emmanuel Giboulet 83

energy expenditure 28
entomologist xi
Entre-Deux-Mers 82, 124
environment xi, xii, 11, 105, 128
environment-friendly 36, 88
environmental stewardship xii, xiii, 41, 44, 47, 64, 88, 92, 99, 102, 105
Eola Hills 48
epilepsy 8
Eppler, John 67
estate-bottled wine 52, 74, 76, 91, 97
Etienne Gonnet 25
Etude du Vignoble de France 98
Eureka 48
Europe 41, 99
European 3; artists 58; clinicians 3; countries 4, 13, 19, x; standards 41; varieties 76; winemaking 60; wines 60
European Federation of Agrobiology Syndicate. *See* F.E.S.A.; Terre et Vie
Exodus 32
expert 50, ix; opinions and ratings 21, 25, 26

F

F.E.S.A. 90; *See also* Terre et Vie
faintness. *See also* sulfites: allergic reactions to
Fairbairn Ranch 51
family 32, 49, 50, 53, 63, 71, 73, 77, 82, 83, 90, 91, 94, 99, 102, 128; setting ix. *See also* Italians: wine-drinking statistics on
farm workers xi
fat 4. *See also* cholesterol
Faust, Serge. *See* Serge Faust
Federal Alcohol Administration Act 18
Federal Association of Organic Viticulture 85
Federal Farm Bill of 1990 12
federal government 17
Felton-Empire Vineyards 55
fermentation 1, 4, 5, 20, 21, 22, 23, 25, 35, 64, 65, 67, 68, 70, 76, 95, 100, 102, 103; barrel 58, 60, 77; inhibition of 25; process 5, 23, 42; secondary 103; superior 25; whole-cluster 68
fertilization 100
fertilizers 71; chemical xi, 4, 16, 17, 28, 73, 75, 86, 87, 94, 96, 97; synthetic 52, 75; synthetically compounded 11
fetal alcohol syndrome 30. *See also* alcoholism
fetal development 31. *See also* pregnancy
fetus 31
Fetzer Vineyards xii, 50

Figiel, Richard xiii
filtering 24, 76; process 20; tight 16
Finger Lakes district 76
fining 14, 48, 76, 100
fish 33
Fitzpatrick, Brian 52
Fitzpatrick Winery 52, 80, 108, 114, 117
Flaherty, Don xi
flashheated 95
flavone factor. *See* vitamin: P
flavor xi, 33, 34, 35, 44, 46, 47, 56, 58,
    60, 61, 64, 66, 67, 68, 69, 72, 73, 74,
    77, 78, 79, 81, 84, 85, 87, 93, 96, 101,
    103. *See also* taste
Florence 93
Florey, Charles 30
Florida 60, 78
flowering cycle 70. *See also* biodynamic
fluidosoufre 19, 41. *See also* sulfur
flushing 17
food ix; intake 6
Food and Drug Administration 17
Ford, Gene ix
foreign substance 1
forest 81; pine 66
Forest Ranch 61, 62
Forestville 77
Forkner, June 2, x
Fort Lauderdale 78
fortified wine 119, 120
Foundation for the Study of Cycles 158
fragile 17
Framingham Heart Study ix
France x, xii, 4, 13, 14, 15, 16, 25, 42,
    67, 76, 81, 89, 94, 97, 98, 102; south-
    ern 83, 88, 91
free-run juice 95
Freiburg 85
French 21, 63, 81; market ix; oak
    barrels 50, 52, 58, 60, 64; oak
    puncheons 56; organic wine 14; wine
    25, 81, 86; expert ratings of 25
French Colombard 33, 54, 63, 119
French Ministry of Agriculture 15
French Revolution 91
Frenkel, Steve 89
Fresno xii
Frey, Jonathan 53
Frey, Paul 53
Frey Vineyards 17, 53, 80, 108, 110, 111,
    112, 114, 117, 119
Frick, Jean Pierre. *See* Jean Pierre Frick

fruit 42, 44, 46, 47, 53, 54, 60, 61, 64,
    66, 67, 69, 70, 78, 84, 86, 87, 95;
    brandies 85; development 96; flavors
    34, 56, 83, 101; wine 23, 69, 70.
    See also Bartlett pear wine; bing cherry
    wine; raspberry wine
fruity 4, 44, 50, 56, 67, 68, 69, 82, 84,
    97. *See also* tasting: notes
full bodied 4, 44, 47, 61, 93, 96. *See also*
    tasting: notes
Fumé Blanc 33, 56, 67, 118. *See also*
    Sauvignon Blanc
fumigants xi
fungi 53, 66
fungicides 28, 77, 100, 103. *See also*
    pesticides

G

Gallo, E. & J. xi
Gamay 33, 75, 76, 113
Gamay Beaujolais 33, 69
game birds 33
garlic 20, 23
gas: inert 64. *See also* bottling practices
gastric acid secretion 3
Gault-Millau 88, 97
Gautière 87
Gavi 86, 128
George Ritchie's Vineyard 55
Gerard Leroux 90
German 81, 85; market ix; style 44;
    wine 127; wine-processing equipment
    43. *See also* Association of German
    Prädikatswein Estates
German Federal Association of Ecological
    Vineyards 100
German Prädikatswein Estates. *See* Association
    of German Prädikatswein Estates
Germany x, xii, 4, 13, 16, 76, 89, 99,
    100, 127,
Gertsch, Franz 59
Gewürztraminer 33, 54, 85, 103, 125
Gier, Theordore 57
Gigondas 87
Gilbert & George 59
Giordano, Albert 74
Giordano, Norma 75
Gironde 90
Givry Blanc 125
Glen Ellen Winery xiii
gold medal. *See* award, gold medal
government 13, 27, 28
Government Warning 26, 27, 38

grand cru Beaujolais Régnié   87
grand cru Morgon   87
Grand Noir   77, 114
Grand vin de Bordeaux   121
Grand Vin du Beaujolais   121
grape: boycotts   xi; fields   xi; production
    xi; ripened   20
Grape Press, The   79
grapes   xi; black   75; Cabernet   88;
    mountain   58
Graves Blanc   124
Graves region   81
Graves Rouge   121
Grenache   63, 84, 88, 94, 97
Grey Riesling   33
Grossblatt, Phil   56
ground-covering greens. *See* cover
    crop; legumes
groundwater   28
growth regulators   11
gruel   102
Guigal La Mouline   98
Guy Bossard   25, 84, 125, 126
Guy Chaumont   82, 123, 125

H

Haas, Robert   94
Hall, Chafee   55
Hallcrest Vineyards   13, 48, 55, 80, 113,
    117, 118
hand tilling   102
hand weeding   102
handcrafted   45
hangover   24. *See also* sulfites: allergic
    reactions to
harvesting equipment   14
HDL. *See* cholesterol: beneficial types
    of; high-density lipoproteins
headaches   x, 17, 72, 91. *See also*
    histamine; sulfites: allergic reactions to
Healdsburg   20, 44
health   129, 158; care facilities   31, 38;
    consciousness   xii; optimal   37
health food beverage   xiii, 106
healthy   xii
heart   x; heavy   32
heart disease   ix, 2, 6; coronary   2, 9, 30;
    ischemic   2, 8; prevention   5. *See also*
    Italians: wine-drinking statistics on
heavy drinkers   30. *See also* alcoholism
herbal sprays. *See* biodynamic: compounds
herbicide–pesticide free   *17*
herbicides   xi, 14, 46, 57, 75, 76, 94, 100,
    102, 103

herbs   34
Hermitage La Chapelle   98
Hess Collection, The   59
Hess Collection Winery   57, 80, 108, 115
Hess Vineyards   57
Hidden Cellars Winery   60, 80, 115
high carbohydrate snack   4
high-density lipoproteins   2. *See also*
    cholesterol: beneficial types of
highland vineyards   29
Hildreth Ranch   60
histamine   4, 7, 24
history   158
History of Wine as Therapy   x
hives   17
Hoesch, Henning   99
Holy Bible. *See* Bible
homeopathic   16
hop kilns   77
hope   158
Hopland   51
hormones   4, 24
hors d'oeuvres   34
horses   44
horsetail   102
hospitals   31
human: being   21; body   1; intellect   155
Humboldt   48, 117, 120
humus   97
hyperuricemia   1. *See also* alcoholism

I

Illinois   60, 92
illnesses   xi
Imbert, Christian   97
immune system   105
importers   ix, xii, 79
independent third party verification   81
industry   xii, xiii; chemical   4, 5; organic
    ix; organic wine   38; profile   xii;
    representatives   27; standards   xiii, 19,
    44, wine   ix, 31, 38, 50, 51, 52, 53
insect: problems   66
insecticides   xi, 14, 25, 57, 76, 96, 100
Institut Œnologique de France   97
insulin   3, 5; secretion   3
integrated pest management (IPM)   50
international   42
interpersonal communication   3, 6
Intervin International Wine Competition   69
intestinal cancers   3
intestines   4, 24
intoxicants   33
intoxicated   4, 5

147

Iowa 92
IPM. *See* integrated pest management
IQs 30
iron 1, 2, 3, 31, 96. *See also* minerals
irrigation 29
Isaiah 32
ischemic heart disease. *See* heart disease:
    ischemic
Islam. *See* Koran
Italian 42, 43, 50, 81; market ix; wines
    85, 86, 127
Italians: wine-drinking statistics on 29
Italy x, xii, 4, 13, 71, 86, 89

J

Japan 4, 44, 89
Javillier, Jean. *See* Jean Javillier
Jean Javillier 83, 125
Jean Pierre Frick 25, 102, 125, 126
Jean-Claude Rateau 25, 83, 123, 125
Jensen, Alfred 59
Jesus 32
Johannisburg Riesling 33, 44, 116, 117
John 32
Johnson, Hugh 97
Joly, A. 96
Joly, Nicolas 16
Jorg Scheel 85
Jougla family 82
Journal of Studies on Alcohol 27
Journal of the American Medical Association
    ix, 7
juice ix, 28, 46, 56, 69

K

Kabinett 101
Kacher, Robert 98
Kaiser Foundation Hospital 31
Kaiser Permanente ix, 30
Kastenbaum, Robert 31
Kermit Lynch Wine Merchants 85
"kidney-hormone". *See* ADH (antiduretic
    hormone)
Kircher Ranch 51
Konrad Estate 116
Koran 32
kosher 3

L

La Coulée de Serrant 16, 94, 95, 96, 126
La Rocca, Phil 62

La Rocca Vineyards 61, 80, 108, 109, 111,
    119
la Sarabande 90, 122
la Suvera 91, 93, 127, 128
labeling 13, 38
Lafite 88
Lancet 9
Languedoc 88
Lapsley, Jim 68
Las Montañas Winery 63, 80, 109, 111
Last Supper 32
late harvested 34, 117. *See also* botrytes;
    rot; sweet wine
L'Atlas du Vin 97
Latour 88
lawmakers 14
Le Bourdieu 82
lead 27, 28, 29, 54, 56; contamination
    28, 29
lead-foil wrappers 28
legislation 38
legumes 67, 77. *See also* cover crop
Leighton, Terrance x
Lemaire Boucher 15
Leoville Lascases 99
Leroux, Gerard. *See* Gerard Leroux
Les Baux Rouge 123
Leviticus 32
life-nurturing xii
light beer 3
lime 62, 96
Linn County 71
liquor x
lithium 4
living xiii, 1, 4, 6, 11, 37, 128;
    components 6; microecology 106;
    universe 37; wine 33, 72, 86, 103, 106
Loire River 95
Loire Valley 84, 96
London Times 88
Longevity 67
longevity 3, 30. *See also* beneficial: effects
Looney, Bill 71
Louis, Morris 58
love 71, 106, 128, 129, 157
Love–Life Principle 158
Loveglo & Comfort 37, 158
low pruned vines 50
low-density lipoproteins 2
Lucia, Salvatore x
Ludwigshöhe 99
Luke 32
lupin 97
Lynch, Kermit 86

M

machinery   28, 29
magnesium   1, 2
Mahaffey, David   46
Maine   60
Maine Organic Farmers and Gardeners
    Association   81
malaria-carrying mosquitoes   xi
Malbec   45
Maler, Leopoldo M.   59
Malvasia   93
manganese   4
manure   77, 98. *See also* fertilizers
Marcel Lapierre   87
Mark   32
market demand   105
Marton, Keith I.   30
Maryland   85, 103
Massachusetts   37
Matthew   32
Matthews, Thomas   96, 100
maturation. *See* aging
Mayacamas Mountains   63
McConnell, Malcolm   29
Mead, Jerry   78
meat   33; dishes   83
Mediterranean Diet, The   29
Mediterranean-style cooking   84
Mendocino County   47, 50, 60, 66, 67; Fair
    55; grapes   60
Mendocino National Forest   54
Mercurey red wine   83
mercury   1
Merlot   33, 44, 45, 56, 61, 63, 67, 76, 82,
    90, 93, 109
metabisulfites   19. *See also* potassium;
    sulfites
metabolism   2
metal   1
méthode ancienne   47
méthode champenoise   84, 90, 92; Brut
    101, 126. *See also* champagne
Meursault   83, 125
Michigan   85
microbiological products   11
microbiologist   x
microbiology   3, 4
microclimate. *See* climate: micro-
microecology   4, 5, 6, 22, 32, 33, 106
microorganisms   29. *See also* microbiology;
    microecology
migraines   4
Mikawa Organic Sweet Rice Brandy   91

mildew   102
Mill Creek   60
mind   105, 106, 158
Mind, Matter, Love and Life   158
minerals   2, 3, 31, 61; absorption of   5;
    chelated   24; trace   2; water-soluble   1.
    See also vitamins: water-soluble
Minnesota   92
Mitchell, Charles   x
Mitoku Organic Brown Rice Sake   91
Mitoku Organic White Rice Sake   91
moderate   ix, 1, 27, 78
Moon   16, 96
mortality rate   ix, 30
mosquito resistance   xi
mothers   30
Motherwell, Robert   58
Mountain Blush   44, 114
mountains   58
Mourvèdre   94
movement   41
Mt. Saint Victorie   99
Mt. Veeder   57, 58, 63
Muhammad   32
mulch: straw. *See* fertilization; fertilizers
mulching   102
Müller-Thurgau   85, 127
multiple regression analysis   30
Muscadet   25
Muscadet de Sèvre-et-Maine   25, 84, 125
Muscat   25, 34, 56, 103
Muslims   32
must   20, 101, 103
mutagen: benevolent   x

N

Napa County   46
Napa Valley   55, 56, 57, 73, 74;
    vineyards   75
National Department of Justice   27
National Federation of Organic Agriculture
    82, 84
natural   13, 14, 16, 19, 20, 24, 33, 34, 43,
    54, 57, 63, 66, 70, 73, 75, 76, 86, 88,
    96, 103, 106; foods   81; winemaking
    103. *See also* fertilizers: natural; sulfites:
    naturally occurring; yeast: natural
Natural Foods Expo East   90
Natural Organic Farmers Association of New
    York   20, 76
Natural Wines Internationale   88
nature   28, 102
Nature et Progrès   14, 15, 81, 82, 83, 84,
    85, 87, 91

naturel 13, 63, 89
nausea. *See* sulfites: allergic reactions to
neo-Prohibitionism 53
nettle plant 96. *See also* biodynamic;
   homeopathic
neuromodulator 24
neurotransmitter 2, 24. *See also* brain-
   chemicals
neutralizing effects 22
Nevada 79
Nevada City 64
Nevada County Wine Guild 64, 80, 110, 116
New England 85
New Jersey 78, 89, 103
New Testament 32
New York 67, 76, 78, 85, 89, 103
New Zealand 51
newborn babies 1
Newton, Isaac 105
ni herbicide 14
ni insecticide de synthése 14
Niellucciu 97
nitrates 25, 28
nitrites 25
nitrogen 48, 49; compounds: synthetic 17
no sulfites added 5, 13, 23, 42, 47, 48, 54,
   56, 62, 63, 65, 72, 73, 74, 76, 87, 88,
   107, 108, 109, 110, 111, 112, 113, 115,
   118, 119, 120, 123, 128
no sulfites detected 70, 82, 110, 115
Noah 32
Noble Companion Port 73, 113
nonalcoholic wine 56
nonirrigated 75
nonleaded aluminum foil 42, 56
Norskog, Tony 64
North Carolina 78
Northwest 69
nouveaux 69, 111
Numbers 32
nursing homes 31. *See also* elderly
nutrient absorption 27, 49
nutrients 1, 2; water-soluble 1. *See also*
   nutrition; nutritional
Nutrients for Love 6
nutrition 105, 158
nutritional 3; value 24. *See also* nutrition

O

oak 47, 96; aging 44, 83; aromas 61;
   barrels 43, 45, 95; American 61;
   French 48, 61, 77, 79; Nevres French
   45, 63; flavor 58, 61, 79. *See also* casks

obesity 3, 6, 157
Octopus Mountain Cellars 66, 80, 110, 114,
   116, 119
odor 23
Oedium 17
offspring 30
OGWA. *See* Organic Grapes into Wine
   Alliance
Ohio 60, 85
Old World style 73
Olson Winery 67, 80, 109, 111, 116, 117,
   118
onions 20, 23
opaque 5
Oppenheim 99
Orange County Fair 61, 65, 78
Oregon 42, 48, 72, 89, 92
Oregon State Fair 72
Oregon Tilth 42, 48
organic 4; certification standards 39, 58,
   67, 76; ethic 41; farming 36, 57, 105;
   growing methods xii, 16, 75, 98, 99, 102;
   market ix; products 106; revolution
   ix; viticulture 66, 94. *See also* organic
   wine; organically grown
Organic Connection, The 37, 79, 129
Organic Food Mail Order Suppliers Directory
   36
Organic Foods Act of 1990. *See* California
   Organic Foods Act of 1990
Organic Grapes into Wine Alliance 14, 39,
   46, xiii; *Newsletter* 105; standards 19
Organic Vintages 89
organic wine: distributors 81; importers 81;
   industry 38; producers xii; representatives xiii
Organic Wine Company, The xiii, 21, 91, 92
Organic Wine Works, The 56, 80, 118, 119
organically grown *11*, 13, 20, 26, 39, 47,
   48, 49, 54, 56, 61, 63, 65, 66, 67, 69,
   70, 88, 97; and processed 24, *26*
organically produced xii
organo-chlorines 13
Orleans Hill Winery 68, 80, 111
Orleans Hill Zinfandel 69
overweight. *See* obesity
oxidation 17, 20, 35, 61
oxidize 20, 68
oxygen 20, 73

P

palatability 3
Parable of the Wicked Husbandmen 32
Paradise 62
Paris 15
Parker, Jr., Robert 47, 88, 95, 98. *See also*
    Wine Advocate, The
Parker's Wine Buyer's Guide 50
parts per billion (ppb) 27, 28
parts per million (ppm) 17, 19, 20, 26, 44,
    46, 54, 56, 65, 70, 73, 74, 78, 80
pasta 33; and wine 84
patients 3
Paton, Dennis 60
Paul, Elizabeth 70
Paul, John 48
Paul Thomas Winery 69, 80, 114
Paul Vineyards 70
peaceful xii
Penfold's Grange Hermitage 98
Pennsylvania 37, 85
Pere et Fils Mercurey 120
Perrin family 94, 95
pesticide: exposure xi; poisonings xi
pesticides xi, 4, 11, 17, 38, 49, 52, 70, 73,
    75, 87, 94, 97, 103, 106. *See also*
    herbicides; insecticides; organic
Petit Roubié 84
Petit Verdot 45
Petite Sirah 33, 66, 74, 77, 78, 114. *See
    also* Syrah
petroleum: byproducts 19; leaded 28
Pfaffenheim 102
Pfeffer family 99
pH 5, 21, 22, 23, 26, 46; low 22, 23
phosphorus 1, 96
physical: affection 1; world 158
physics 158
physiology 1
Picolit 93
Picpoul de Pinet 84, 124
Pierre Frick. *See* Jean Pierre Frick
Pierrette Rateau 83
Pievescola di Casole d'Elsa 93
Pievescola, Italy 93
Pinot Blanc 33, 103, 125
Pinot Gris 103
Pinot Meunier 85
Pinot Noir 33, 42, 46, 47, 48, 50, 54, 56,
    65, 66, 72, 74, 77, 82, 83, 85, 109, 123
plant 11
plastics. *See* additives
political reform 36

Ponderosa Vineyards 71, 80, 110, 113,
    115, 120
poor countries 4, 5
Pope John Paul II 54.
Pope Julius II 93.
port 34, 73, 108, 113. *See also* dessert
    wines
Portland 48
Porto-Vecchio 97
Portugal 4
potash 96
potassium 1, 2; bisulfite 19; metabisulfite
    19, 45. *See also* sulfites
powder preparations. *See* biodynamic:
    compounds
ppb. *See* parts per billion (ppb)
ppm. *See* parts per million (ppm)
Prager, Jim 73
Prager Winery and Port Works 73, 80, 113
Prager Winery Bed and Breakfast 74
predators: natural 105
pregnancy 27, 30, 31
prescribing 6
preservation xiii
preservatives xi. *See also* additives; sulfites
pressing 95
price ranges 107
prime viticultural region 66
processing 1, 12, 24, 29, 54, 67
producers: U.S. ix; classification of U.S. 80
production ix
Products Compliance Division 70
proper use x, xii, 2, 27, 37, 106
protein 1, 3, 4; absorption 3. *See also*
    amines
Provence 25, 87, 98
Proverbs 32
pruning 71, 100
Psalms 32
psychobiology 158
psychology 91, 158. *See also* mind
public: education xiii, 36, 157; service 158
Puget Consumers' Co-op 69
Puligny-Montrachet 25, 125; white 83
pumps 100; centrifugal 65, 100
Puyallup 69

Q

Qualitätswein mit Prädikat 85, 101
quality 11, 18, 21, 25, 26, 42, 45, 49,
    51, 65, 70, 100, 128; handling 5;
    higher 21, 22, 24, 25, 51
quantum mechanics 158

151

Quebec 78
quercetin x
Quran. *See* Koran

R

RDA. *See* recommended daily allowance
racking 76, 95, 103
rain 71
Rango Rosso 91, 93, 127
Raskin, Veronique xiii, 15, 91
raspberry wine 69. *See also* fruit: wine
Rateau, Jean-Claude. *See* Jean-Claude Rateau
Rateau, Pierrette. *See* Pierrette Rateau
Recent Developments in Alcoholism 30.
recommended daily allowance 2
recyclable 56
recycled glass 42, 61
red wine x, 1, 3, 4, 5, 17, 19, 22, 24,
    33, 34,54, 65, 72, 73, 82, 83, 90, 94,
    95, 107, 112, 127; aging 22; blend 56,
    84; country 87; dry 3, 4, 5, 22; serving
    33; table 33, 54, 72
Red Zinfandel Nouveau 68
Redford, Myron 42
Redwood Valley 51, 60, 67
Redwood Valley Home Ranch 51
Regnie 121
renin 1
Reno 79
research ix, 36
residual: gas 69; sugar 103
residue analysis 13
resistance xi
Restaurant Wine 47
restaurants 38
retention 5
retirement communities. *See* nursing homes
Rheinhessen 101, 127
Rhineland Palatinate 99
Rhône 95, 99
Rhône-style red 77, 114
Rhône Valley 99
rhubarb wine 69, 70
Richard, Charles 44
Riesling 55, 60, 77, 85, 101, 103, 125;
    Dry 44; Estate White 55. *See also*
    Johannisburg Riesling; Grey 33; off-
    dry 77; White 33, 47, 55, 66, 117
Ripperdan Ranch xii
Ritchie, George. *See* George Ritchie's Vineyard
rivulets 5
Robert Haas Selections 94
Robert Kacher Selections 98
rock phosphate 62

Rocky Mountains 71
Rosé d'Anjou 90
Rosé de Loire 90
rosé wine x, 3, 23, 90, 92, 97, 99, 114,
    124
Rossi Ranch 79, 112
rot 102. *See also* botrytes; dessert wines;
    sweet wine
Roussanne 94
Roussanne-Cuvée Vieilles Vignes 95
Royal Escort Port 74, 113
Ruby Cabernet 108
Russian River Vineyards 77, 116. *See also*
    Topolos at Russian River Vineyards
Russian River watershed 54

S

"S" Bianco 93
Safers soap. *See* beneficial: insects
safety issues 36, 51
Saint-Chinian Rosé 124
Saint-Chinian Rouge 120
sake 89, 91
salmon 33
San Colombano 93
San Francisco 36, 70, 91
San Francisco Chronicle ix, 50, 69
San Francisco State University x, 2
Sangiovese 93
San Pietro Vara Vineyard and Wine Company
    13, 74, 80, 112, 113
sans engrais chimique 14
sans fongicides 14
sans produits chimiques 14
Santa Cruz Mountains 55, 117
Santa Rosa 31
Saumur 90
Sauvignon Blanc 33, 44, 45, 48, 51, 52,
    54, 55, 69, 72, 77, 82, 117; Late Harvest
    54. *See also* Fumé Blanc
Savenniéres 95
Scheel, Jorg 85
Scheuermann's classification 101
Scheurebe 101, 127
schnapps 85
Schumacher, John 56
Sciaccarellu 97
Scotland 30
Seattle Times 44, 52, 54, 66
Seattle, Washington 69
seaweed. *See* fertilizers: natural
Section 26569.11. *See* California Health
    and Safety Code; California Organic Foods
    Act of 1990

sediment: naturally occurring 21, 24, 26, 72
Sekt 101
self-esteem 3
semi-organic methods. *See* herbicide–pesticide free; transitional
Semi-Sweet Aperitif–Satisfaction Plus 72, 120
Sémillon 33, 45, 55, 56, 82, 119
Seneca Lake 76
senses 4
Serge Faust 85, 126
serving suggestions 34
Sevé 44, 119
Shelter Cove 48
sherry: cream 34; dry 3, 22. *See also* appetizer wines
Shoemaker, Wells 28
shortness of breath. *See* sulfites: allergic reactions to
side effects. *See* additives; sulfites: allergic reactions to
Siena hills 93
Siena, Italy 93
Sierra Dreams 52, 114
Sierra Nevada: foothills 52; mountains 61
silicon 2. *See also* minerals
Silvaner 101
silver medal. *See* award: silver medal
Silver Thread Vineyard 76, 80
sinusitis. *See* sulfites: allergic reactions to
sleep 3, 31; sound 6
smell 5
Smith, Rod 50
smokestack filters 19. *See also* sulfur dioxide: petroleum-derived
snacks 34
SO₂. *See* sulfur dioxide (SO₂)
social 158; enjoyment ix, 31; responsibility 36, 38
society ix, 105
Society of Medical Friends of Wine 37
Society of Wine Educators 37
sodium: bisulfite 19; metabisulfite 19. *See also* potassium; sulfites
soil 11, 28, 45, 61, 62, 72, 77, 86, 98, 101; fruitful 102; healthy 29; limestone 103; pine forest based 66; tests 16; type 45; volcanic 43, 61
Solano County 46
solar power 29, 66
Solar System 16
Sonnenbrunnen Winery 85, 127
Sonoma County 44, 49, 77, 78, 112, 116
Sonoma Harvest Fair 78

soup 34
Spain 4
Spanish wine 4
sparkling wine 19, 33, 34, 35, 48, 77, 82, 84, 90, 120, 126; domestic 120; French 126; serving 35. *See also* champagne; méthode champenoise
Spätburgunder Rotwein 85, 127
Spätlese 101
special natural wine 34
spectroscopic analysis 1
spirits 2
spirituality 32, 161
spoilage 23, 35
St. Helena 73
stabilizing agents 14
stainless steel tanks 43
standards 11, 48, 100; highest quality 106; prohibited 14
state: law 16
steam-clean. *See* sterilization methods
Steffano Bellotti 86, 128
Steiner, Rudolf 16
Stella, Frank 58, 59
sterilization 5
sterilization methods 17
stimulating 3
Stockley, Tom 44, 52, 54, 66
stomach 32; upset x
storage 72; containers 14; proper 35; temperature 54, 61, 100; ideal 35
Story of Wine and Its Uses, The 33
Streissguth, Ann 30
suckering 71
sugar xi, 3, 5, 20, 21, 22, 23, 29, 46, 49, 70, 101, 103; content 5, 22, 23, 26, 70. *See also* additives
sulfite: content 5, 21, 24, 26; forms of lead 28; sensitive 42, 63
sulfite-free. *See* sulfites: no detected
sulfites xi, 5, 13, 17, 19, 20, 23, 24, 26, 49, 50, 72, 76, 80, 128; allergic reactions to 5; detectable 70; detected 49; metabolization of 24; natural content of 73; naturally occurring 20, 76; no detected 20, 42, 82. *See also* no sulfites added
sulfur 23, 96, 98, 100, 103; elemental 57; mined 19; non-processed powdered 96, 97; organic 23. *See also* no sulfites added
sulfur dioxide (SO₂) 4, 19, 20, 41, 67, 95; petroleum-derived 19; pure 19. *See also* sulfites
sulfur-copper 94. *See also* sulfur

Surgeon General   27
Sutter Home Winery   xii
sweet wine   20, 22, 72; white still   34. *See also* botrytes; dessert wines; ports
sweetness   5, 34, 73, 102. *See also* taste
Switzerland   16
Sylvaner   103, 126
symbols. *See* certification: symbols
synthetic, treating agents. *See* additives; pesticides; preservatives; sulfites
synthetically compounded   *11*, 19
Syrah   54, 55, 84, 87, 94, 98, 99, 112, 123; Cabernet Sauvignon blend   88. *See also* Petite Sirah; Sirah-Syrah.

T

table wine   3, 33, 65, 74, 90, 91
tables   11
Tainted Booze   x, 36
Talmage   60
tannic acid   5
tannins   5, 22, 33
tartrate crystals   24
taste   4, 5, 23, 47, 66, 67, 68, 73, 76, 81, 83, 89, 95; bitter   20; complex   4, 58, 60, 68, 73, 76, 78, 81, 87, 103; preferences   33. *See also* senses
tasters   55
tasting   25, 55, 58, 67, 74, 78, 81; notes   107
Tawny Summer Port   74
TBA. See Trockenbeerenauslese
Technology of Wine Making, The   22, 24
Tehana County   63
temperature   34. *See also* storage: temperature; room. *See* storage: temperature
tension   1, 6
tension-reducing   3
terms   11
Terre et Vie   14, 15, 84, 85, 90
Terry Theise Selections   94, 99
Texas   85, x
Theise, Terry   99
therapeutic   2
Third World   4, xi
Thomas, Paul   69, 70
Thompson, Howard   56
Thuaud Vin Mousseux de Qualité   126
tillers   28
Tillman Vineyard   60
Tokaj   93
Tokay Pinot Gris   25
Topolos at Russian River Vineyards   77, 80, 112, 113, 114, 116, 118

tractor   45
tranquilizing   3
transition   46
transitional   16, 57, 67, 72; period   12, 16
transparent   5
Trebbiano   93
Trockenbeerenauslese   101, 102
Tulare County   xi
Tuscany   93
types   11, 33, 34
tyramine   3

U

"U-shaped" curve   30
U.N.I.A.   14, 15, 83
Ukiah   48, 51, 60
Ultimo   112
"Uncork the Magic"   53
Underground Wine Journal, The   78
underweight   3. *See also* eating disorders
unfiltered   49, 52, 63, 87, 95
Union Nationale Interprofessionelle de l'Agrobiologists. *See* U.N.I.A.
United Farm Workers of America   xi
United States (U.S.)   ix, 4, 15, 17, 19, 37, 41, 44, 54, 66, 70, 76, 80, 81, 89, 91, 92, 107; Congress   26; grape growers   39; organic wine producers   14, 41; wine producers   xii, xiii, 13
University of Angers   15
University of California   x, 51
University of Dundee   30
unrefined   49, 95
uric acid disorder   1. *See also* alcoholism
urine   1

V

valerian   96. *See also* biodynamic: compounds; homeopathic
Valley Oaks   51
Valley Oaks Ranch Vineyard   51
value   25, 47; system   92
Vaslin press   77
vasodilation   1
Verband Okologisches Weinbau   101
vermouth   34
vetch   97
Vignoble de la Jasse. *See* Domaine de la Jasse
Vin Blanc   66, 119
Vin d'Alsace   126
Vin de Pays   84, 87, 121
Vin Rosé   72, 115
vinaigre   *21*

vinegar 21
vinification 16
Violes 87
vitamin: B x; B-complex 1; B$_1$ 4, 24;
 C 2, 4, 20, 24; P x,2, 3, 24
vitamins: water-soluble. *See* nutrients
Vosges foothills 102

W

Wall Street Journal, The 54
warning label 17, 26
Warszawa 8
Washington 12, 43, 78, 89, 92
Washington, D.C. 36, 85, 103
Washington Times 85
water resources: preservation of 50
watery 5
wealthier countries 4
weddings 78
weed control 62
weeding 96
weedkillers 16, 96
weight 3; problem 5
Weingut Brüder Dr. Becker 99, 127
Weingut Günter Wittmann 99, 101, 127
Weisser Riesling *Kabinett* Trocken 101
West Coast 41
West Coast Wine Competition 61, 79. *See
 also* award-winning wines
Westhofener Aulerde Riesling Extra Brut
 Sect 101
Westhofener Kirschspiel Scheurebe
 Spätlese 101
Westhofener Mörstein Riesling *Spätlese*
 Halbtrocken 101
Westhofener Mörstein Riesling *Spätlese*
 Trocken 101
Westhofener Steingrube Albalonga
 Beernauslese 101
Westhofener Steingrube Albalonga
 Trockenbeerenauslese 101
Weygandt–Metzler Importing 101, 102
White Riesling. *See* Riesling: White
white wine x,3, 17, 33, 34, 93, 95, 115,
 118,127, 128; aging of 22; Burgundy
 83; dry 4, 88; fine 22; oak-aged 82;
 Riesling 33, 47, 55; semi-dry 56;
 serving 33, 34; Zinfandel 56, 63, 119
Whitten, David N. 31
whole food 3, 6
Widman, Les and Lil 74, 75
Wiegand, Ron 47
Wild Horse Valley 46, 115

Wild Rose 66, 114
Williamette Valley 71
Wine Advocate, The 47, 98. *See also* Parker,
 Jr., Robert
Wine and Health x
Wine and Spirits 97
Wine and Your Well-Being x
Wine Guild International Wine Tasting 78
Wine Institute, The 33, 38
Wine Magazine 25
wine saver 72
Wine Spectator, The xi, 55, 64, 96, 100
Wine Trader, The 78
winebiber 32
winemaking 19, 20, 22, 26, 32, 37, 44, 45,
 49, 53, 54, 55, 60, 62, 63, 70, 73, 74,
 103. *See also Technology of Wine Making*
winery: certification 13; small 74; solar
 powered 66
Wisconsin 92
women 27, 30. *See also* pregnancy
world 158
World Health Organization xi, 10
world wars 4
wounds 32

Y

yeast 14, 16, 20, 86, 103; cultured 76;
 native 73; natural 49, 76; wild ix,
 48
yields 46, 47, 51, 58, 94, 98, 100

Z

zinc 1, 31. *See also* minerals; nutrients;
 vitamins: water-soluble
Zinfandel 33, 50, 51, 54, 56, 60, 63, 64,
 65, 67, 68, 69, 74, 75, 76, 77, 78, 79,
 111; botrytes 63; grapes 62; Sparkling
 White 56; White 69
Zodiac constellations 96. *See also*
 biodynamic; cycles

About the Compiler

Robert Johnson received his bachelor of science degree from Arizona State University in 1985 and has continued his research endeavors in the biological sciences. His particular focus has been on optimizing health by means of nutrition and organic foods, which led to copublishing several books on those topics. Over the past five years, Robert has spoken as an expert on organic foods at public and academic events, has appeared on public education television, and has written a monthly "Organic Update" column for a local community newspaper for the past three years. In addition, he currently manages a community service educational organization, which publishes and distributes a variety of literature and books on the topic of organic foods and serves as a network for environmental and health organizations around the country.

Robert feels that he is representative of many individuals who have had failing health and were fortunate enough to have discovered the healing and life-nurturing properties of organic foods and the concept it is based on, that love nurtures life. At the height of Robert's academic career, he suffered from an ulcer, bulimia, obesity (50 pounds heavier than present), borderline diabetes, depression, and a shrinking social circle. When his friend and later partner introduced him to organic foods and an understanding about nutrition, Robert's ailments gradually disappeared. Today he is living testimony to the health benefits of organic food and wine and desires to make that information available to those who have had similar problems with little or no hope of overcoming them. When asked his greatest inspiration, he responds, "Love is self-rewarding, a gift that awaits those who explore its awesome and healing power."

About the Editor

Richard Pasichnyk has taken a completely interdisciplinary approach to more than seventeen years of study in the biological and physical sciences and history to uncover the underlying basis of unified theory. His recent articles in *Cycles*, a publication of the Foundation for the Study of Cycles, reveal the mechanism behind solar and lunar cycles in earthquakes,* climate, and war,** and as a result, he has astounded leading scientists in many disciplines with his new model of the Earth. His extensive research has led him far beyond present-day understandings in physics, astrophysics, geophysics, quantum mechanics, plate tectonics, history including ancient history, psychology, psychobiology, and many other fields. One such understanding that has emerged from Richard's research is nutrition's role in optimizing health. In a book on nutrition, Richard describes how it is possible to optimize health, as well as eliminate most if not all disease or disorder states, simply by understanding how the mind and body work and interact with one another, and applying the "Love–Life Principle" of nutrition. Simply stated, the Optimum Love–Life Principle involves the concept of foods produced with the nurturing—love—of life in mind. His forthcoming publication, *Mind, Matter, Love and Life* uncovers the role of the collective conscious and unconscious minds in the social and physical worlds. Scientifically confirmed, this book offers answers, and therefore hope, toward making the world a better place for all. Richard is currently preparing several publications, and serves as editor of Loveglo & Comfort Publications, an information-based public service organization. If you would like to be notified of future publications, please write to Loveglo & Comfort, Post Office Box 88, Tempe, Arizona 85280.

---

* Solar and Lunar Cycles in Earthquakes: An Electrostatic Trigger. *Cycles* 41:305-312. (1990)

** The Solar-Terrestrial Linkage in Climate and War: Part I: Climate. *Cycles* 42:125–133. (1991)

The Solar-Terrestrial Linkage in Climate and War: Part II: War. *Cycles* 42:316–322. (1991)

Producer, Importer, and Distributor Address and Phone List

Amity Vineyards
18150 Amity Vineyards Rd., S.E.
Amity, OR 97101-9603
(503) 835-2362

Badger Mountain Vineyard and Winery
110 Jurupa
Kennewick, WA 99337
(509) 627-4986, or (800) 643-WINE

Bellerose Vineyard
435 West Dry Creek Road
Healdsburg, CA 95448
(707) 433-1637

Blue Heron Lake Winery
503 Hunt Street
Napa, CA 94559
(707) 257-0647

Briceland Vineyards
5959 Briceland Road
Redway, CA 95634
(707) 923-2429

Cameron Winery
8200 Worden Hill Rd.
Dundee, OR 97115
(503) 538-0336

Chartrand Imports
P.O. Box 1319
Rockland, ME 04841
(207) 594-7300, or (800) 473-7307

H. Coturri & Sons
P.O. Box 396
Glen Ellen, CA
(707) 525-9126

Fetzer Vineyards
P.O. Box 611
Hopland, CA 95449
(707) 744-1250

Fitzpatric Winery
7740 Fairplay Rd.
Somerset, CA 95684
(209) 245-3248

Frey Vineyards
14000 Tomki Rd.
Redwood Valley, CA 95470
(707) 485-5177

Hallcrest Vineyards
379 Felton Empire Rd.
Felton, CA 95018
(408) 335-4441

Hess Collection Winery
P.O. Box 4140
Napa, CA 94558
(707) 253-2131

Hidden Cellars Winery
P.O. Box 448
Talmage, CA 95481
(707) 462-0301

Kermit Lynch Wine Merchants
1605 San Pablo
Berkeley, CA 94702
(510) 524-1524

LaRocca Winery
13505 Helltown Rd.
Chico, CA 95928
(916) 891-8872

Las Montañas Winery
4400 Cavedale Rd.
Glen Ellen, CA 95442
(707) 996-2448

Natural Wines Internationale
1411 E. Jackson
Phoenix, Arizona 85034
(602) 894-2997

Nevada County Wine Guild
11372 Winter Moon Way
Nevada City, CA 95959
(916) 265-3662

Octopus Mountain Cellars
P.O. Box 613
Boonville, CA 95415
(707) 895-3718

Olson Winery
3620 Rd. B
Redwood Valley, CA 95470
(707) 485-0323

Organic Vintages (California)
P.O. Box 832
Ukiah, CA 95482
(707) 463-2304, or (800) 877-6655

Organic Vintages (New York)
Somerstown Turnpike, Rt. 100
Somers, NY 10589
(914) 276-3854, or (800) 877-6655

Organic Wine Company
54 Genoa Place
San Francisco, CA 94133
(415) 433-0167

Orleans Hill Winery
P.O. Box 1254
Woodland, CA 95695
(916) 661-6538

Paul Thomas Winery
1717 136 Place, N.E.
Bellevue, WA
(206) 747-1008

Paul Vineyards
3661 Road J
Redwood Valley, CA 95470
(707) 485-0814

Ponderosa Vineyards
39538 Griggs Drive
Lebanon, OR 97355
(503) 259-3845

Prager Winery and Port Works
1281 Lewelling Lane
St. Helena, CA 94574
(707) 963-7678

Robert Haas Selections/Vineyard Brands
Haywood Road
Chester, VT 05143
(802) 875-2139

Robert Kacher Selections
3015 V Street, N.E.
Washington, DC 20018
(202) 832-9083

San Pietro Vara Vineyard & Wine Co.
1171 Tubbs Lane
Calistoga, CA 94515
(707) 942-0937

Silver Thread Vineyard
6075 Sirrine Rd.
Trumansburg, NY 14886
(607) 387-5721

Terry Theise Selections/Milton Kronheim
2900 V St., N.E.
Washington, DC 20018
(202) 526-8000

Topolos at Russian River Vineyards
5700 Gravenstein Hwy
No. Forestville, CA 95436
(707) 887-1575

Triple B Wines (Mail Order)
1021 Oyster Bay Road
East Norwich, NY
(516) 922-6613

Weygant–Metzler Importing
P.O. Box 56
Unionville, PA 19375
(215) 932-2745